CATALOG OF THE
JOHANNES HERBST COLLECTION

CATALOG OF THE JOHANNES HERBST COLLECTION

Edited by Marilyn Gombosi

The University of North Carolina Press • *Chapel Hill*

PREFACE

The Archives of the Moravian Church in America contain approximately ten thousand musical documents dating from the eighteenth and nineteenth centuries. A large part of the archival material consists of manuscript copies of music performed in American Moravian communities during that period. Included among the manuscripts are collections of sacred vocal music used by the various congregations in Pennsylvania, Ohio, and North Carolina and libraries of orchestral and chamber music performed by the *collegia musica* that flourished in each of the settlements. The collections that belonged originally to the Pennsylvania and Ohio congregations have been deposited in the Archives of the Moravian Church in Bethlehem, Pennsylvania. Documents pertaining to music in North Carolina Moravian settlements are housed in the headquarters of The Moravian Music Foundation, Inc., in Winston-Salem, North Carolina.

One of the functions of The Moravian Music Foundation is to direct the cataloging of the Moravian music archives. This volume is the first in a series of thematic catalogs being prepared under the auspices of The Foundation. Its completion was made possible by the aid and advice of Donald M. McCorkle, former Director, and Ewald V. Nolte, present Director of The Foundation; Vernon Nelson, Archivist, and Lothar Madeheim of the Moravian Archives in Bethlehem, Pennsylvania; Miss Grace Siewers and Mrs. John Eggleston, Archivists of the Moravian Archives in Winston-Salem, North Carolina; and Stephen Gombosi. The cataloger owes a special debt of gratitude to her assistant, Miss Patricia Harry.

THE JOHANNES HERBST COLLECTION

The Johannes Herbst Collection of music manuscripts, preserved in Winston-Salem, North Carolina, was selected for the initial cataloging project because its accessibility is of utmost importance to further progress in Moravian music research. Even the preparation of this catalog has contributed significantly to present knowledge of the origins of the art-music traditions of the Moravian church. It has answered many questions and opened avenues for further research.

The Collection was part of the personal library of the Moravian minister and musician, Johannes Herbst (1735-1812), and remained in his possession until his death. After Herbst's death, the Collection was deposited in the Moravian Archives in Salem, North Carolina. At that time, the Collection consisted of 464 manuscripts containing scores of approximately one thousand anthems and arias for use in Moravian worship services, i.e., the Congregation Music (A), scores and/or parts for forty-five extended vocal works (B), and a few volumes of miscellaneous pieces (C).

Herbst had arranged in numerical order the manuscripts of Congregation Music; recently-discovered scores in his hand which belong in the category of service music have been assigned numbers surrounded by brackets and have been added at the end of the original Collection, beginning with number [465]. The extended works were unnumbered and had been scattered among other collections in the archives. These have been retrieved, arranged in alphabetical order by composer, and supplied with Roman numerals to avoid confusion with the numbering system of the Congregation Music.

Only six manuscripts are missing from the Congregation Music, and recent experiences suggest that the lost scores may be found as the inventory of the music archives progresses. The state of the extended works is less satisfactory, but lost parts and missing pages may yet be recovered. The Collection is in excellent physical condition; only two manuscripts are defective. On some pages, the ink has bled through the paper to some extent, but the scores are legible.

The Herbst Collection stands apart from the rest of the music archives in a number of ways. It was privately owned and largely unused while the congregation libraries were community property and subject to constant use. Many music copyists contributed at various times to the libraries of the different congregations, but the Herbst Collection was prepared almost entirely by Herbst himself. The congregation libraries contain individual parts that were used in performances in the local communities; the Herbst Collection, however, consists almost entirely of musical scores. Congregation libraries, then, were practical working collections in contrast to the Herbst Collection which was compiled as a reference library. Many of the same compositions appear in the Herbst Collection and in the various congregation libraries, but the latter are limited by their locales, reflecting the tastes and performance practices of the individual American Moravian communities. The Herbst Collection is limited only by the life span of its owner. Its range covers the whole Moravian sacred music tradition through the sixty years of its most vigorous growth—from its inception in the mid-eighteenth century to its maturity in the first decade of the nineteenth century.

MUSICAL PRACTICES IN THE EIGHTEENTH-CENTURY
MORAVIAN CHURCH

The hymn tradition of the *Unitas fratrum*, later known as the Moravian church, can be traced back to the year 1501, when the Society in Czechoslovakia published the first Protestant hymnal.[1] Forced underground during the Counter Reformation, the Unity of Brethren continued to print Czech, Polish, and German hymnals. In the early part of the eighteenth century, the Society regrouped in Herrnhut, Germany, under the protection of Count Nicholas Ludwig von Zinzendorf, a devout Lutheran. Zinzendorf, a prolific hymnwriter, encouraged the Moravians to develop a strong musical tradition.[2] Under his leadership, the hymns and liturgies of the Moravian church were organized and their use in the various worship services was specified by church officials.[3]

The origins of the art-music tradition of the Moravian church are not clear at the present time, since there has been little intensive music research conducted in the archives in Herrnhut. In America, the earliest clues found by this writer consist of manuscript pages in the Bethlehem Archives which give the text for a *Cantata auf die Einweihung des ledigen Brüder-hauses zu Bethlehem, am 6. Dec. 1744* (Cantata for the Dedication of the Single Brothers' House in Bethlehem, on Dec. 6, 1744) and a poem for the Christmas Eve Vigils held in Bethlehem in the same year. Various stanzas of the Christmas Eve poem are designated as recitatives, arias, and choruses; the musical setting has not been located,

1. The 1501 hymnal, containing the texts of approximately eighty hymns, is preserved in the Prague Museum in Czechoslovakia. A microfilm copy in the Archives of The Moravian Music Foundation, Inc., Winston-Salem, N.C., is being used to prepare metrical translations of the texts and to identify the melodies to which the texts were sung. At the present time, melodies for twenty of the hymns have been found; these are adaptations of Gregorian melodies.

2. James David Nelson, *Herrnhut: Friedrich Schleiermacher's Spiritual Homo land* (Ph.D. dissertation, University of Chicago, 1963), gives lengthy and detailed descriptions of a typical day, week, month, and year in eighteenth-century Herrnhut, based on documents preserved in the Archives of the Moravian Church, Bethlehem, Pa. The important position music held in the everyday lives of the Moravians is stressed.

3. An official memorandum issued in June, 1753, to Peter Boehler concerning his journey to America specifies that "for Song Services *(Singstunden)* and special church occasions, the small hymnal *(Das kleine Brüder-Gesangbuch)* will be used. For the Sunday Preaching Service and Congregation Days, one is to avail oneself of the large hymnbook *(Alt- und Neuer Brüder-Gesang)* and Part II of the Elegantien, the small Shepherd's book *(Hirten-Lieder von Bethlehem)*, and also the small Sunday or Sharon book *(Der Gesang des Reigens zu Saron)*." The English translation is supplied by Albert F. Jordan, who discovered the memorandum in the Archives of the Moravian Church, Bethlehem, Pa.

but the poetic meters and rhyme schemes suggest that the stanzas could have been sung to existing chorale tunes and thus would not have required special musical settings. A set of compositions for solo voices and instrumental ensembles by Johann Daniel Grimm are the earliest examples of the art-music tradition known to this writer. These compositions, some of which are dated as early as 1750, are preserved in the Winston-Salem Archives.

The first systematic effort to provide art-music for Moravian worship services apparently was made by Christian Gregor, the Moravian minister and musician who later compiled the official Moravian hymnal (*Gesangbuch,* 1778) and its companion tune-book (*Choralbuch,* 1784). Gregor states in his autobiography[4] that he began in 1759 to compose or adapt pre-existent music for performances on anniversaries of the church[5] and other special events. Among the several gatherings held on such occasions, the most ambitious musical offering was the Ode presented during the Lovefeast[6]—a fellowship meeting usually held in the afternoon, during which a simple repast was served.

The text for a Lovefeast Ode[7] was compiled from Biblical passages, hymns, and original verses pertinent to the occasion. Prescribed scriptural texts—the Daily Texts[8]—for the day on which the Ode was to be

4. Autograph copy in Archiv der Brüder-Unität, Herrnhut, East Germany; microfilm copy in the Archives of the Moravian Music Foundation, Winston-Salem, N.C. A slightly different memoir is printed in *Nachrichten aus der Brüder-Gemeine,* Gnadau, 64.Jahrgang, Oktober, 1882, I., 865-903, and *Beiträge zur Erbauung aus der Brüder-Gemeine,* Christian Frederick Stückelberger, ed., Gnadau, 2.Jahrgang, I., 427-478; copies of the *Nachrichten* and the *Beiträge* are preserved in the Archives of the Moravian Church in America, Southern Province, Winston-Salem, N.C. English translations of both memoirs are given in Jane Stuart Smith, *Christian Gregor: A Critical Edition of His Autobiography and a Contribution to the Study of Autobiographical Writings of the 18th Century Pietists* (Ph.D. dissertation, The University of North Carolina, 1962).

5. A listing of the principal anniversaries peculiar to the Moravian church year is given on page xxi of this volume.

6. The regular Sunday Preaching Service usually included the performance of an anthem in addition to the sung liturgies and hymns. The Song Services *(Singstunden)* were informal meetings devoted primarily to the singing of hymns, although special music was performed occasionally, especially when visitors to a settlement were present. Handwritten daily records of music performed by the choir at each service were kept in booklets, a few of which are preserved in the Archives of The Moravian Music Foundation.

7. Odes were sometimes entitled Psalms, Festal Psalms, or Cantatas; musical distinctions between these forms are not clear.

8. A *Loosung (Losung)* and *Lehr-Text* for each day of a particular year were chosen by lot (hence the use of the term *Loosung*) two years in advance. These were printed in booklets and sent to all Moravian congregations. The *Losung* was drawn from the Old Testament and the *Text* from the New Testament. With each Biblical passage was printed a hymn verse which elaborated upon the meaning of the Scripture. The Moravian Church still issues annually the Daily Text Book for each year.

presented were usually included among the various texts used in the Ode. Printed copies[9] of the Ode text were distributed to the congregation, which played an active role in its performance.

Christian Gregor's musical settings of Lovefeast Odes are cast in recitatives, arias, duets, and choruses with instrumental accompaniment,[10] interspersed with congregational singing of chorales. Other Moravian musicians such as Herbst and Johann Christian Geisler followed Gregor's example, compiling musical odes for the principal dates of the church year and special occasions. They borrowed freely from each other's works as well as from other Moravian and non-Moravian sources and adapted the borrowed material to fit their particular needs. An example of the extensive borrowing and adaptation techniques used by these composers can be found in the music for November 13, 1767 (A 96): works by Pergolesi and Handel, adapted by Herbst, are joined with earlier compositions by Gregor and new anthems by Geisler and Herbst in order to form a complete service consisting of seven anthems, with added written directions that specify the chorales to be sung by the congregation.

The composition of musically-unified Odes initiated by Christian Gregor began to disappear toward the end of the eighteenth century. Odes were still performed at Lovefeasts, but music directors in each settlement drew their settings from miscellaneous compositions in the existing choral repertory.[11] The music libraries of the American

9. If printing facilities were not available, the school children were expected to make the necessary number of handwritten copies. See *Records of the Moravians in North Carolina* (Raleigh, N.C., 1922-), VI, 2741.

Judging from the numerous references in the *Records* to the preparation, distribution and performance of Lovefeast Odes, their presentation was a matter of great concern to the church officials who periodically reviewed the current practices and issued new directives to those who were responsible for overseeing the preparations.

10. Although specific directions for the performance of an Ode are given on the printed text and in the musical setting, circumstances sometimes forced the Moravians to violate those directions. On September 19, 1780, in Bethabara, N.C., John Frederik Peter not only played the organ accompaniment—probably a keyboard reduction of the orchestral parts—for an Ode, but also "sang the parts arranged for the chorus." Jacob Loesch performed the same feat in Bethania, N.C., on September 7, 1782. See *ibid.,* IV, 1628, 1832.

11. Proof of this practice came to light in recent years when this writer was attempting to locate the music for the Lovefeast Ode performed at the first formal commemoration of Independence Day held in Salem, N.C., on July 4, 1783. After months of searching, the anthems were found in widely-separated manuscripts in the Salem Congregation Collection. Two recitatives and a duet, presumed lost, were discovered two years later in a box of miscellaneous manuscript fragments in the Lititz Congregation Collection, now housed in the Archives of the Moravian Church, Bethlehem, Pa.

Moravian settlements contain few examples of complete musical Odes. The use of Daily Texts in musical settings continued unabated, but younger Moravian musicians tended to compose them as single anthems or arias with instrumental accompaniment.

Johannes Herbst lived in the right places at the right times to observe the early music tradition as it was formed by Gregor, and to record the subsequent changes in Moravian musical practices.

JOHANNES HERBST

Johannes Herbst[12] was born on July 23, 1735, of Lutheran parents residing in Swabia. At the age of seven, he was sent to Silesia to live with an uncle who had embraced the Moravian faith. The following year, Herbst entered the Moravian school for little boys in Herrnhut, Germany, the center of Moravian activity during the eighteenth century. The boy exhibited a strong musical talent at an early age and soon he was playing the organ and helping with other musical activities in Herrnhut while serving an apprenticeship in clockmaking.

Giving up his apprenticeship in 1748, Herbst moved to Neusalz and for the next fourteen years he lived in various German Moravian settlements, including Gnadenfrey, Gnadenberg, and Kleinwelke, before returning to Herrnhut. These were years of crisis—the "Sifting Period"—in the Moravian church and Herbst's biographer credits him with easing the critical situation with his "musical talents as well as other merits."

From 1762 to 1766, Herbst lived in England while working in the children's schools established there by the Moravians. On his return to the Continent, he lived first in Kleinwelke and then in Herrnhut before moving to Barby where he was ordained a Deacon of the Church in 1774. After his ordination, he was assigned to Neudietendorf for six years. He spent another six years in Gnadenfrey and then emigrated to America with his wife, the former Rosine Louise Clemens. His three children—Sophie Louise, Johann Ludwig whose compositions are found in this Collection, and Samuel Heinrich whose early death in 1786 is commemorated in one of his brother's compositions (B XIX)—were left in Germany to be educated in the Moravian schools.

On his arrival in America, Herbst went first to Lancaster, Pennsylvania, where he was ordained a Presbyter of the Church on October

12. Information about Herbst's life in Europe is based on a handwritten biography of unknown authorship, preserved in the Archives of the Moravian Church, Winston-Salem, N.C. Apparently Herbst did not follow the Moravian custom of preparing a memoir (Lebenslauf) to be read at his funeral. Additional materials concerning Herbst's years in America are found in the Diaries of the Lititz Congregation for the years 1786-1812, filed in the Archives of the Moravian Church, Bethlehem Pa.

15, 1786; in addition to his church duties in Lancaster, Herbst served as a trustee of Franklin College during the time that James Buchanan, the future President of the United States, was chairman of the board of trustees. A few years later (1790), Herbst was a member of the distinguished group of citizens, including George Washington and members of Congress, who were invited to participate in the dedication ceremonies of Zion Lutheran Church in Philadelphia, then the nation's capital. While living in Lancaster, Herbst often traveled to Lititz, Pennsylvania, to direct the music at special church festivals. For the dedication of the new church edifice on August 13, 1787, Herbst directed the choirs and orchestra in a performance of his dedication anthem (A 333) and presided at the new organ built by the Moravian, David Tannenberg.

In 1791, Herbst moved to Lititz where he remained for almost twenty years, serving first as assistant pastor and then as pastor of the Congregation. He led an active life in Lititz, fulfilling his pastoral duties, leading worship services, directing the music and playing the organ when necessary, keeping the official Diaries, Minutes, and Financial Accounts of the Congregation, traveling with his musicians to various towns in Pennsylvania to provide special music for important events, composing anthems for special days in the Moravian communities, and copying music for use in the Moravian schools. In addition to these activities, Herbst found time to catalog the Lititz Congregation music library and to prepare performers' parts for approximately five hundred compositions; these parts remain in the Lititz Collection where they form a major part of the Congregation library.

In 1811, Herbst was transferred to Salem, North Carolina. Two days before his departure from Lititz, he was consecrated a Bishop of the Moravian church. Bishop Herbst served as pastor of the Salem Congregation only a few months before he was stricken with his last illness. Despite his advanced age and ill health, he remained actively interested in the music of the church during his short tenure in Salem, contributing manuscripts of performing parts to the Congregation library and making corrections in the catalog of that library which had been prepared in 1808. Johannes Herbst died in Salem on January 15, 1812. In recognition of the esteem in which Herbst was held outside the Moravian communities as well as within, the Elders' Conference took the unusual action of instructing one of its members to contact a Raleigh, North Carolina, printer and ask that "the home-going of our departed Brother, Johannes Herbst, shall be announced in a suitable manner in the public papers."[13]

13. *Records of the Moravians in North Carolina*, VII, 3172.

HISTORY OF THE COLLECTION

During his sojourns in the various European Moravian communities, Johannes Herbst had ample opportunity to select and make copies of the compositions he wished to own. He began copying the earliest art-music of the church composed by Gregor and Geisler, and continued to add to his Collection those compositions that interested him. Following the first four manuscripts in the Collection which contain liturgies and one anthem by Gregor from the year 1752, Herbst arranged the scores in chronological order, beginning with the music for *Christnacht* 1758 and 1759 (A 5) and continuing through the music for the year 1779 (A 214). Apparently these manuscripts were copied while Herbst lived in Europe and had access to the sources for his Collection.

In America, Herbst was cut off from these sources and, forced to make copies of whatever music he could borrow, he could no longer continue the systematic organization of his Collection. If compositions from earlier years became available to him, he added copies of these works to his library with little regard for chronology. Undated compositions, often groups of works by a single composer, were copied as they were received. Thus, only a rough chronology is apparent in the second half of the Collection.

Correspondence between Herbst and Jacob van Vleck,[14] a fellow minister and musician who was serving as principal of the girls' boarding school in Bethlehem, Pennsylvania, sheds light on the manner in which Herbst managed to continue the expansion of his Collection while living in America. In a letter sent to Van Vleck from Lancaster on September 4, 1790, Herbst mentions that he has recently made a copy of the quartet from E. W. Wolf's *Ostercantate* (B XLI, XLIII) and is at work on the choruses from *Athalia* by J. A. P. Schulz (B XXXVII). He asks to borrow the Hymns of Schulz (B XXXVIII) and any new Congregation Music which Van Vleck may have acquired during his recent trip to Europe. Herbst's request apparently was granted for, on August 8, 1791, he mentions that he still has the Hymns and, on October 25, 1791, he notifies Van Vleck that he is returning the Congregation Music which had been loaned to him. Unfortunately, no record has been found that notes what Congregation Music was sent to Herbst at that time. However, a memorandum prepared by Van Vleck on February 29, 1792, lists another group of compositions which were being sent to Herbst. Herbst's copies of the sixteen compositions on the list are found in the Collection with the following numbers: A 201.1b; 213.2b; 234.1; 265;

14. The Herbst-Van Vleck correspondence is preserved in the Archives of the Moravian Church, Bethlehem, Pa.

272b; 301.2; 312; 315.1; 317.1; 321; 351.1, 2, 3; 359.1, 2, 3.

On January 1, 1793, Herbst writes that he is returning the Schulz Hymns but that he has not yet finished copying *Athalia.* The following month, on February 27, he sent a copy of *Athalia* to Van Vleck, quoting his copying fee as £ 3.39. Evidently, Herbst made one copy for hire and another for his personal library. The numerous references to copying fees in the Herbst-Van Vleck correspondence suggest that Herbst was hired to copy music for use in the school's music curriculum.

THE BOOK OF TEXTS

In a letter from Herbst to Jacob van Vleck dated March 6, 1792, Herbst refuses Van Vleck's request for a catalog of his Collection, saying that there is only one copy which he uses constantly so that he cannot part from it. It is so extensive that he cannot promise when he can make a copy to loan to Van Vleck.

The catalog in question is probably the companion volume to the Collection that was filed in the Salem Archives along with the scores after Herbst's death. A bound volume measuring 18 x 24 centimeters, the book contains the complete texts for all of the Congregation Music, arranged in the same numerical order as the manuscripts. The basic number for a manuscript stands above the group of texts used in the manuscript; the texts for separate compositions within the manuscript are preceded by a secondary number which usually corresponds to the secondary number on the manuscript. Consistently in the first half of the volume and sporadically thereafter, the basic number is followed by an inscription giving the date, and frequently the place and event, for which a composition was prepared, e.g., *"333. Zur Einweyhung des neuen Kirchensaals in Lititz am 13. Aug. 1787."*

The first two entries in the book of texts are not in Herbst's hand and do not use German script. The remainder of the texts are in script, and numbers 3 through 455 are definitely in Herbst's writing. A marked change in handwriting occurs with number 456 and continues through the final entry, number 464. The firm, neat strokes which characterize Herbst's clear hand are lacking; the letters are wavering and ill-formed. It is not possible at this time to determine if an aged colleague completed the book of texts for Herbst or if the last entries were made by Herbst shortly before his death.

In the margins of the volume, frequent notations in red ink indicate the specific location of the same text in another part of the volume, e.g., *"Vid. No. 13,9/ pag. 5"* or simply refer to the register of texts

("*Vid. Reg.*") for the same purpose. The register of texts, placed at the end of the volume, is an alphabetical arrangement of brief text incipits which are followed by page and number references.

There is no index of the composers who made the musical settings of the texts. When he began his Collection, Herbst seems to have been unconcerned with the identification of composers. In particular, he neglected to credit Christian Gregor as the compiler of the musical Odes that comprise a large part of the first quarter of the Collection. Consequently these Odes had been considered the work of an unknown musician until Gregor's identity was established during the course of this project; at that time, the significant position these compositions hold in the history of Moravian Church music was realized. Herbst had attached Gregor's name only to the few compositions by Gregor which were added to the Collection after Herbst came to Amercia.

The first composer named in the book of texts is Johann Christian Geisler ("*di Geisler.*" Nos. 12; 20; 39; 40; 42; 47-49) followed by Herbst himself ("*di Herbst.*" Nos. 78; 81). The composer citations in this part of the volume appear to be later additions to the book of texts, for they are positioned after the basic number in such a manner as to suggest that they had been squeezed into whatever space was available. After the entry for No. 81, ample room beside the basic number was allotted for the composer's name. There are instances, however, in which the space has not been filled in and the citation beginning "*di*" is then left blank. If the musical setting of a text is the work of two persons, both names are given in the citation; if the corresponding manuscript contains music by more than one composer, the composer's name is given beside the text which he set.

The book of texts has been of invaluable assistance in the preparation of this catalog.

THE MANUSCRIPTS

Considering the number of years which were spent in amassing the Collection, the manuscripts of the Congregation Music exhibit a surprising uniformity in size and handwriting. Few of the manuscripts vary more than a centimeter from the 18 x 24 cm. norm. Johannes Herbst copied all of the scores except for the few which were given to him, and his distinctive script remained remarkably unchanged over the years. The consistent manner in which he formed clef signs and notes makes his script the most easily identifiable in the music archives. The staves are drawn by a rastral and slight curves in the individual staves suggest that the rastral was drawn freehand across the page.

The following score order is used consistently in the manuscripts:

Brasses	Trumpets
	Horns
	Trombones
Woodwinds	Flutes
	Oboes
	Clarinets
	Bassoons
Strings	Violin I
	Violin II
	Viola
Voices	Soprano
	Soprano (or Alto)
	Alto (or Tenor)
	Bass

Organ, Fondamento

The staves for the basic ensemble of voices and strings are not labeled on the scores unless a composition demands extra parts or the ensemble is used in an unusual manner. Parts for flutes and horns—the most common additions to the basic ensemble—are sometimes left without designation, but all other instruments are named beside their respective parts at the beginning of a manuscript. The bottom stave is often undesignated, but it may carry various labels, e.g., *Fundamento, Fondamento, Funda., Fondam., Org. or Orgel.* The term given on the manuscript has been retained in this catalog.

If a title page is present, it contains the inscription that appears beside the corresponding basic number in the book of texts. Titles of compositions are rarely given. A signature of ownership, *"Johannes Herbst"* or *"Joh. Herbst,"* is placed in the lower right-hand corner of the title page. If there is no title page, the inscription is placed above the score on the first page of music and Herbst's signature is found at the bottom of the page.

CATALOGING PROCEDURES

Each manuscript in the Collection has been cataloged in the following manner:

1. *Composer, adapter, compiler*
   Composer credits given by Herbst on the manuscript or in the book

of texts have been retained in this catalog. Since adaptations are sometimes credited by Herbst to the original composer and, at other times, to the adapter, it is possible for the same composition to be listed under different composers. In such a case, Herbst's designation is kept, but the original source of the material (if known) is cited in the explanatory notes following the description of the music. In the index of composers, the manuscript number will be found under the names of both composer and adapter, and, if the manuscript is compiled by another individual, he is credited in the index also.

The identity of composers who were not cited by Herbst has been established by checking the same composition in other manuscript collections in which composers' names are given. Information derived from these sources was accepted if it appeared on a manuscript dating from the same period as the Herbst manuscript. Later sources, such as late nineteenth-century manuscripts, were not considered reliable.

In certain instances, a tentative identification has been established by circumstantial evidence gathered from eighteenth-century catalogs of congregation libraries in which the particular manuscript needed for comparison could not be located. When the evidence seemed strong enough to warrant the tentative identification, the composer's name has been given, preceded by a question mark. If the evidence was not conclusive, the composer entry is marked [Unidentified].

Immediately following the composer's name and dates, the inscription on a manuscript denoting the date, place, and event for which the composition was prepared appears in italics. An inscription which pertains to only one composition within a manuscript appears in italics in the description of that composition.

2. *Title*

Since titles are rarely given on the manuscripts of Congregation Music, the initial words of the text have been used as standard titles and enclosed in brackets. When possible, the wording used in the title register of the book of texts has been followed. Compositions that consist of two or more independent musical sections are given compound titles in which the initial words of each section are supplied, separated by dashes. Such sectional treatment of a composition usually indicates that the texts of the separate sections are taken from different sources. Idiosyncracies in spelling and grammar have been retained without comment.

Titles given on the extended works are transcribed faithfully, with the ends of lines marked by diagonal strokes. Since some of these manuscripts may be copies of published editions, the positioning and wording of a title page may be significant in identifying the model from which Herbst worked.

3. *Musical incipit*

The opening phrase of the first violin part has usually been transcribed; this part usually anticipates in the instrumental introduction the principal vocal line that follows. If the vocal part differs significantly from the violin line, it is given also, following the first excerpt and separated from it by /\/\/ . For sectional compositions, the first phrase of each section is given in order of appearance, separated from each other by a double bar. Treble or bass clefs have been substituted for C clefs.

4. *Description of the music*

A period and dash separate the various parts of the description:

a. *Performance medium.* The vocal and string parts are identified by the clefs used: Treble, Soprano, Alto, Tenor, Bass. An unmarked part in the treble clef placed above the first violin part is identified as a flute part; an unmarked part calling for a transposing instrument is assumed to be a horn part. This procedure was established after consulting marked performing parts of the same compositions in other manuscript collections. If the ensemble is divided into contrasting groups, the parts are listed in groups separated by a diagonal stroke, e.g., S/SSAB indicates a soprano part separate from the rest of the vocal parts; or S;Fl/SSAB;Str indicates that a soprano and flute are used as a group against the vocal and string ensemble. The various families of instruments are separated by semicolons.

b. *Key.* The basic key of the composition is given, without reference to brief modulations. Key changes between large musical sections of a composition are noted and separated by semicolons.

c. *Tempo and expression markings.* Indications for tempo and expression are transcribed literally from the manuscript. Brief changes are not noted. Changes in markings between large sections of a composition are given, separated from preceding markings by semicolons.

d. *Length of composition.* For the Congregation Music and compositions cataloged separately in the extended works, the length of the composition is given in the number of measures. In the extended works, the number of extant pages is given.

e. *Sources of texts and tunes.* The identification of texts used in the first quarter of the Collection was made difficult by the fact that the early composers compiled texts from single phrases from various parts of the Bible and brief quotations from hymns; these were then arranged in a logical sequence of thought and used as the text for a composition. Many times, one phrase could have been given a number of different attributions because it appears in many places in the Bible and is also used as the opening phrase of a hymn. Slight alterations in the wording of a scriptural passage have strained the resources of the Biblical concordance. While the text references given in the catalog for the problematical texts have been carefully checked, there are no doubt some errors and omissions. The references given for Biblical texts are based on the German Bible.

A complete set of hymn collections in use during the eighteenth century was not available for this project, so that the source of a number of hymns could not be traced. Hymn quotations also presented a problem in identification because many of these quotations begin in the middle of a stanza. Some were located by searching through all of the available hymns in the same meter, others were discovered by chance, but the majority were not found. If a hymn could not be located, it is designated only by the word "Hymn."

A hymn which has been located is designated by hymn number and verse, separated by a comma. The name of the author in parentheses follows the reference. "Zinzendorf" refers to Nicholas Ludwig von Zinzendorf; his son, Christian Renatus, is designated by his initials. The principal source used for hymn identifications was Johannes Herbst's personal copy of Gregor's *Gesangbuch zum Gebrauch der evangelischen Brüdergemeinen,* (Barby, 1778), containing Herbst's notations in the margins which give the names of hymn authors. Other hymnals which yielded information are: *Das Gesangbuch der Gemeine in Herrnhuth.* [Herrnhuter Gesangbuch] *2. Aufl.* (1737); *Zugaben* (1741); *Das kleine Brüder-Gesangbuch. Dritter Theil, enthaltend eine abermalige Sammlung alter und neuer Verse* (Barby, 1767); and *A Collection of Hymns for the Use of the Protestant Church of the United Brethren* (London, 1789). If a hymn could not be located in the Gregor hymnal but was found in one of the other hymnals the source is given in abbreviated form enclosed in brackets immediately after the hymn number.

If a chorale tune is used in a composition, it is identified by the number assigned to it in Gregor's *Choral-Buch, enthaltend alle zu dem Gesangbuche der Evangelischen Brüder-Gemeinen vom Jahre 1778 gehörige Melodien* (Leipzig, 1784). This numbering system established by Gregor is still in use.

f. *Measurements.* Since there is so little variation in the dimensions of Congregation Music manuscripts, it seemed unnecessary to indicate the exact size of each score. These figures are available in the card catalog at The Moravian Music Foundation. The sizes of manuscripts of extended works vary considerably, however, so the dimensions of these manuscripts have been given.

g. *Explanatory notes.* Written indications on the manuscript which do not fit in any of the above categories are transcribed in italics and enclosed in quotation marks. Miscellaneous information pertaining to the manuscript or to the music is given in ordinary type.

When pertinent, references have been made to other manuscripts in the Collection which utilize the same music. These references are given as a temporary substitute for the finding index which will constitute the last volume in this series; the finding index will include all themes found in all the music collections in the Moravian Archives.

The original plans for this catalog called for a listing of some early American performances of compositions found in the Herbst Collection. As the project developed and several scores in the Collection were compared with the performing parts actually used in the American Moravian settlements, it became evident that musicians in each town adapted compositions to fit the musical tastes, functional requirements, and available personnel in the particular community. Under these circumstances, it was felt that listing American performances of a composition without noting all of the many deviations from Herbst's version would be inaccurate and misleading; on the other hand, if all variant versions were noted, the lengthy list of deviations would prove more confusing than helpful in determining the performance practices of the separate Moravian settlements. Thus, it was decided that this volume would give only Herbst's own notations concerning the date, place, and event for which a composition was prepared. In subsequent volumes of this series, the catalog of each settlement's music library will describe a composition as it was actually used in performances held in that settlement; the reader will be referred to the corresponding Herbst manuscript so that he may make his own comparisons of the various versions of the composition.

Marilyn Gombosi
The Florida State University
April, 1969

PRINCIPAL DATES IN THE MORAVIAN CHURCH YEAR

The Moravian church observes a number of anniversaries and memorial days in addition to the holidays observed in all Christian churches. The special days include commemorations of important events in the history of the church and anniversaries of the separate groups, called Choirs, within the total congregation. The congregation, historically, was divided into Choirs according to age, sex, and marital status. The following list of special days includes those which appear in the Herbst Collection:

January 10—see July 9
January 12—see July 9
February 2—The Presentation of Christ in the Temple
March 25—Festival of all the Choirs
April 30—Widows' Choir
May 4—Unmarried Women's Choir (Single Sisters)
May 12—Adoption of the Brotherly Agreement and Statutes (Herrnhut, 1727)
June 4—Older Girls' Choir
June 24—see July 9
July 6—Martyrdom of John Hus (1415)
July 9—Older Boys' Choir [alternate days are listed]
July 14—see August 17
July 25—see August 17
August 13—Spiritual Baptism of the Church (Herrnhut, 1727)
August 17—Children's Choir [alternate days are listed]
August 29—Unmarried Men's Choir (Single Brothers)
August 31—Widowers' Choir
September 7—Married People's Choir
September 16—see November 13
October 21—see July 9
November 13—Formal Promulgation of the Doctrine of the Immediate Headship
      of Jesus Christ in His Church.

CONTENTS

Zum grossen Sabbath
1768.

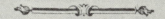

Chorus.

Du der mit Blut und Wunden
Bedeckt vom Kampfplatz kam,
Und nach den Arbeits-Stunden
Die Ruh im Grabe nahm,
Wir sinken bey Dir nieder,
Und Herz und Auge fließt;
O ihr erblaßten Glieder,
Seyd tausendmal gegrüßt!

Gemeine.

Wir sind Deinem Tod verpflicht't, bis der letzte Kuß
geschicht.

Chorus.

Siehe, das ist GOttes Lamm, das der
Welt Sünde trägt.

Solo.

Christe, Du Lamm GOttes! der Du trägst
die Sünde der Welt,
Erbarm dich unser!
Christe, Du Lamm GOttes! der Du trägst
die Sünde der Welt,
Gib uns Deinen Frieden!

Gemeine.

Ich stehe da und weine, und freu mich, daß ich bin'
und werde Friedens-Scheine aus JESU Leiden inn':
Wenn ich auf Augenblicke die Herrlichkeit könnt' sehn;
ich säh' doch bald zurücke auf Seine Leidens-Schön'.

)(
Chorus.

*Printed Text of the Lovefeast Ode Presented on
Great Sabbath, 1768*

\90.) ... 17.. Aug. 1767. di Geisler.

1.) ...

2.) ...

Oder:

...

3.) ...

\91.) ... 29. Aug. 1767.

1.) (di Geisler) Lobt den Herrn, ... Gott loben, ... Vid. N.º 92.
...
Hallelujah!

2.) (di Herdt) ... Vid. N.º 92.
...

\92.) ... 29. Aug. 1767. di
Lobt den Herrn, ... Gott loben, ... Vid. N.º 91.
...
... Lobt den Herrn.

Page from the Book of Texts

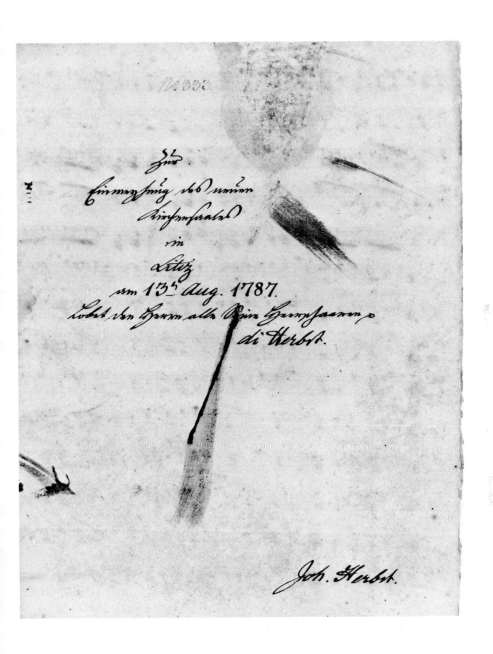

Johannes Herbst Collection, Ms. 333, Title Page

Johannes Herbst Collection, Ms. 333, Score

Resting Place of Johannes Herbst in God's Acre,
  the Moravian Graveyard, Winston-Salem, North Carolina

CATALOG OF THE
JOHANNES HERBST COLLECTION

A. Congregation Music
in the Johannes Herbst Collection

1   ?GREGOR, CHRISTIAN (1723-1801) *Ordinations-Liturgien*

1.1   [Herr unser Gott]
Zur Acoluthen-Annahme

SSAB.-B-Flat maj.-64m.
At end: *"Gem. Weil man es thun darf, so wünscht man dir"*

1.2   [Herr, Herr Gott]
Zur Ordination zur Diaconie

SSAB.-B-Flat maj;G min.-52m.

1.2b   [Lob sey deiner heiligsten]
Doxologie nach der Ordination

SSAB.-B-Flat maj;E-Flat maj.-19m.

1.3   [Von Gottes Gnaden]
Zur Ordination der Prediger

SSAB.-B-Flat maj.-64m.

1.4 [Von Gottes Gnaden, die in den Schwachen]
  Zur Ordination der Bischöfe

SSAB.-B-Flat maj.-93m.

2 ?GREGOR, CHRISTIAN (1723-1801) *Trauungs-Liturgie*
  [Herr, Herr Gott der du]

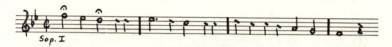

SSAB;keyboard(mel,bass).-B-Flat maj.-54m.
Pts: Canto I,II,A,B;keyboard.

3 GREGOR, CHRISTIAN (1723-1801) *Zu Weynachten 1752 di Gregor*
  [Siehe, ich verkündige euch grosse Freude]

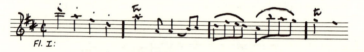

S;2Fl;Str.-D maj.-*Vivace.*-77m.-Lucä 2:10,11.
For another setting, see Herbst [3b].

[3b] [Siehe, ich verkündige euch grosse Freude]

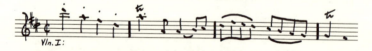

SSAB;Str.-D maj.-*Vivace.*-77m-Lucä 2:10,11.
For another setting, see Herbst 3.

4 GREGOR, CHRISTIAN (1723-1801)
  [Gelobt seyst du der du sitzest]
  Bibel-Gesang: Gelobt seyst du der du sitzest über Cherubim

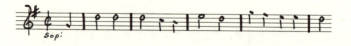

SATB;2Hns;Str.-G maj.-206m.-*Eingang 1* [*Liturgische Gesänge...*, 1793]
See Herbst [468.1].

5   GREGOR, CHRISTIAN (1723-1801) *Zur Christnacht 1758 und 1759*

5.1   [Jungfräulichs Kindgen]
        Ariette 1.

SSB;Str.-G maj.-56m.
Pts: Canto I,II,B;Vln.I,II,Vla,Basso.

5.2   [Ave Christ-Kindlein]
        Ariette 2.

SSB;Str.-G maj.-*Lebhafter.*-40m.
Pts: Canto I,II,B;Vln.I,II,Vla,Basso.

6a   GREGOR, CHRISTIAN (1723-1801) *Losung am 21. Febr..1759*
        [Der Herr liess Aron—Der Herr segne dich]
        Der Segen

SSAB;Str.-B-Flat maj;E-Flat maj.-*Gravitaetisch.*-67m.-
IV.Mose 6:23-26.
For parts, see Herbst 7[.7].
For a solo version of *Der Herr segne dich,* see Herbst 6b.

6b   GREGOR, CHRISTIAN (1723-1801)
        [Der Herr segne dich]
        Der Segen

S;Str.-E-Flat maj.-*Sempre piano. Gravitaetisch.*-35m.-
IV.Mose 6:24-26.
On back of ms., skeleton pt. for Clavicembalo, in D maj.
For a choral version, see Herbst 6a.

7   GREGOR, CHRISTIAN (1723-1801) *Charfreytags Music 1759.*
        in 6 Arien

7.1   [Ach was wandelt unsre Seelen]
        Aria 1.

SSAB;Str.-E min.-29m.-Hymn.
Pts: Canto III(Alto);Vln.I,II,Vla,Basso.

7.2   [O Handlung voller Majestät]
        Aria 2.

?;Str.-F maj.-30m.-Hymn.
Pts: Vln.I,II,Vla,Basso.

7.3   [Wiederholts mit süssen Tönen]
        Aria 3.

?;Str.-G maj.-32m.
Pts: Vln.I,II,Vla,Basso.

7.4   [Heiliger Herre Gott!]
        Chorus 4.

SSAB:Str.-F maj.-13m.-Hymn 1464(Litany); Tune 519.
Pts: Canto III(Alto);Vln.I,II,Vla,Basso.
See Herbst 29.1

7.5   [Ey noch einmal!]

SSAB;Str.-D maj.-16m.
Pts: Canto III(Alto);Vln.I,II,Vla,Basso.

7.6   [Da sind wir arm und blöde]

?;Str.-B-Flat maj.-17m.
Pts: Vln.I,II,Vla,Basso.
For alternate text, see Herbst 64.3: *"Mein Freund der weiss und rothe."*

7[.7]   [Der Herr liess Aaron—Der Herr segne dich]
Kirchen-Segen. Zur Losung am 21. Febr. 1759.

SSAB;Str.-B-Flat maj;E-Flat maj.-67m.-IV.Mose 6:23-26.
Pts: Canto III(Alto);Vln.I,II,Vla,Basso.
For score, see Herbst 6a.

8   GREGOR, CHRISTIAN (1723-1801) *Zum 4, May 1759*

8.1   [Wie köstlich sind für uns]

SSAB;Str.-B-Flat maj.-*Etwas langsam, doch lebhaft.*-37m.-
Psalm 139:17; I.Corinther 2:9,10.
See Herbst 14.5.
At end: *"Choral: O mein Herr Jesu Christ..."* [Hymn 1262]

8.2   [Höre Tochter schaue drauf]

SSAB;Str.-B-Flat maj.-*im vorigen Tempo.*-37m.-Psalm 45:11,12.
At end: *"Choral: Wir dank'n mit 1000 Thränen"*

8.3   [Es sollen wol Berge]

SSAB;Str.-B-Flat maj.-*Moderato.*-56m.-Jesaia 54:10.
Optional ending on separate sheet.
See also Herbst 29.4, first section.
At end: *"Choral: 1. O er bleib uns eingedrückt...*[Hymn 467],
2. Wir grüss'n uns...[Hymn 1089]"

8.4   [Glück zu wie gut]

SSAB;Str.-B-Flat maj.-*Munter.*-42m.-Hymn 1315 (Zinzendorf).
At end: *"Choral: Wir dankens. . ."*
        "No. 5: Wünschet Jerusalem Glück" [Herbst 22.10?]
        "Choral: 1. O das erfreuet uns...;
        2. Unds — bleibt; 3. Die stehen einer jeder..."

9   GREGOR, CHRISTIAN (1723-1801) *Zum 17. Aug. 1759*

9.1   [Das saget der Heilige]

SSAB;Str.-A maj.-*Lebhaft moderat.*-20m.-Offenbarung 3:7.
At end: *"Choral: Ist das mein lieber Bruder"* [Hymn 1186]

9.2   [Vor dir, habe ich alles]

SSAB;Str.-A maj;B min.-*In vorigem Tempo.*-15m.
At end: *"Choral: Meine Armuth ist nicht zu ergründen"*

9.3   [Die Leute sollen dich]

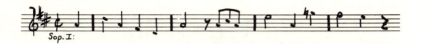

SSAB;Str.-D maj.-*In vorigem Tempo.*-29m.-Offenbarung 3:9,var.
At end: *"Choral. Da sehet nur..."*

9.4   [Du hältst die Passions-Geschichte]

SSAB;Str.-D maj.-*Im vorigen Tempo.*-25m.
At end: *"Choral. Das lieblichste Gedichte..."* [Hymn 167]

9.5   [Darum will ich dich]

SSAB;Str.-D maj.-*Muntrer.*-29m.-Offenbarung 3:10,var.
See Herbst 13.9.
At end: *"Choral. Da sollen die Unwürdigen..."*

9.6   [Wer überwindet, den will ich]

SSAB;Str.-G maj.-*Gravitaetisch.*-52m.-Offenbarung 3:21,var.
At end: *"Choral: Hilf Gott, wie herrlich..."* [Hymn 941]

10   GREGOR, CHRISTIAN (1723-1801) *Zum 17. Aug. 1760*

10.1   [Dieses mein Haus]

SSAB;2Fl;Str;Fondamento.-G maj.-*Lebhaft, doch serieux.*-98m.

10.2   [Er wird einen Samen]

SSAB;2Fl;Str;Fondamento.-G maj.-*Gravitaetisch.*-39m.-Psalm 22:31.

10.3   [Deine Kinder werden dir geboren]

SSAB;2Fl;Str;Fondamento.-F maj.-*Mässig munter.*-76m.-Psalm 110:3.

11   [UNIDENTIFIED] *Zu dem Geburts-tage der C. Mar. v. Zinzendorff am 6. Nov. 1760*

11.1   [Zu der Zeit da der Grund]

SSAB;Str.-C maj.-*Moderato.*-48m.-Sacharja 8:9.
Losung for Nov. 6, 1760.

11.2   [Das heilsam Gottes-Wort]

SSAB;Str.-C maj.-*Etwas Munterer.*-30m.

11.3   [Kommt lasst uns]

SSAB;Str.-C maj.-*Etwas weniges langsamer als voriges.*-22m.

11.4 GREGOR, CHRISTIAN (1723-1801)
[Du bist kommen zu dem Berge Zion]

SSAB;Str.-C maj.-*Mässig, lebhaft.*-65m.-Ebräer 12:22-24.

12 GEISLER, JOHANN CHRISTIAN (1729-1815) *Gemeintags Psalm, zum 22. Dec. 1760*
[Nun danket alle Gott]

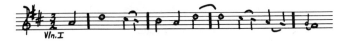

SSAB;Str.-D maj.-[no tempo marking at beginning] ;*Andante; Frölich.*-50m;64m;56m.-Hymn 1611,var.
P.4: quotation from Tune 146, 4-pt. harmonization.

13 GREGOR, CHRISTIAN (1723-1801) *Zur Christnacht 1760*

13.1 [Der Friede-Fürst kommt]

SSAB;Str.-A maj.-*Moderato.*-21m.

13.2 [Tenor Recit:] *Siehe, ich komme* [Ebräer 10:7]

13.3 [Du Hirte Israel höre]

SSAB;Str.-A maj.-*Andante.*-60m.-Psalm 80.2.

13.4 [Tenor Recit:] *Siehe, ich will mich*

13.5 [Ach dass du den Himmel]

SSAB;Str.-D maj.-*Lebhaft, doch nicht zu geschwinde.*-31m.-Jesaia 64:1.
For an SS setting, see Herbst 67.1 (Geisler).

13.6   [Tenor Recit:] *Es ist noch ein kleines dahin* [Haggai 2:7]

13.7   [Herr ich warte auf dein Heil]

SSAB;Str.-A maj.-*Angenehm. con Sordini.*-Hymn 221(Nachtrag).-17m.
For alternate text, see Herbst 14.12: *Und Sein Name;* Herbst 37.3:
Ave o du blass...; Herbst 42.9: *Er wird bey Ihnen wohnen;* Herbst
48.3: *Wer mich liebet.*

13.8   [Tenor Recit:] *Bald wird kommen* [Maleachi 3:1]

13.9   [Siehe, ich verkündige euch grosse Freude]

SSB;Str.-D maj.-*Munter u. ein bisgen geschwind.*-30m.-Lucä 2:10,11.
See Gregor's *Darum will ich dich,* Herbst 9.5.

13.10   [Ehre sey Gott in der Höhe]

SSAB;fig.bass.-D maj.-*Lebhaft.*-43m.-Lucä 2:14.
For an SSAB;Str. version, see Herbst 22.3. For SSAB;Str/SSAB;
Str. version, see Herbst 97.11.

13.11   [Seht wie freundlich]

SS;Str.-G maj.-*Arioso.*-76m.

13.12   [Ich kann vor Liebe]

SSAB;Str.-G maj.-*Munter.*-33m.

14   GREGOR, CHRISTIAN (1723-1801) *Zum 4. May, 1761*
       Praelud:

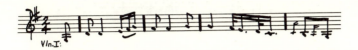

Str.-G maj.-*Andante.*-58m.
At beginning: "*NB. Bey Besezung doppelter Stimmen, oder wo Flöten zu haben sind, spielt ein Theil um eine Octav hin u. da höher.*"

14.1   [Tenor Recit:] *Siehe, alle Seelen*

14.2   [Zion hörts—Dis ist der Tag]

SSAB;Str: "*NB kan auch ohne Instrumente gesungen werden.*"-G maj.-*Lebhaft.*-33m.-Psalm 97:8; 118:24.

14.3   [Vor dir ist Freude]

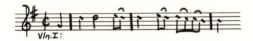

SSAB;Str.-G maj.-*Angenehm.*-34m.-Psalm 16:11.
For a version with 2 Horns, see Herbst 64.2.

14.4   [So spricht der Herr: Dis Volk habe ich]

T;Str.-Recit;Arioso.-G maj;B-Flat maj.-39m.-Jesaia 43:21; Jeremia 29:11.

14.5   [Wie köstlich sind für uns]

SSAB;Str.-B-Flat maj.-*Munter.*-69m.-Psalm 139:17; I.Corinther 2:9,10;
Psalms 100:3; 118:23; 106:2.
For another version, see Herbst 8.1.

14.6   [Freue dich und sey fröhlich]

SSAB;Str.-B-Flat maj.-*Munter, doch nicht zu geschwinde.*-55m.-
Sacharja 2:10; Psalm 68:5; V.Mose 31:6; Jesaia 65:24.
See Herbst 114.1.

14.7   [O wie ist die Barmherzigkeit—Wer hätte gedacht]

SSAB;Str.-F maj; G min.-34m.-Psalms 119:156; 33:4.

14.8   [Siehe da eine Hütte Gottes]

SSAB;Str.-E-Flat maj.-*Gravitaetisch und alles gestossen.*-33m.-
Offenbarung 21:3; Psalm 84:2; Sprüche 8:31; Jesaia 57:15.

14.9   [Siehe der Bräutigam kommt—Ja, schmecket und sehet]

SSAB;Str.-F maj;B-Flat maj.-*Lebhaft; Etwas munterer.*-90m.-
Matthäi 25:6; 28:20.

14.10   [O Herr! du erforschest—Du erfreuest uns]

SSAB;Str.-B-Flat maj.-53m.-Psalms 139:1; 8:5; 21:7; Hohelied 2:3;
Psalms 63:9; 35:10.
Contains musical excerpts from Herbst 13.7: *Herr ich warte...*

14.11   [Der Herr ist mein Theil]

SSAB;Str.-B-Flat maj.-*Lebhaft.*-100m.-Klaglieder 3:24.
Contains chorale, *Herzlich lieb hab ich dich* (Hymn 689,Tune 232).
For an adaptation by J. C. Geisler, see Herbst 80.6.

14.12   [Da sind wir worden—Sie sind Jungfrauen—Und Sein Name]

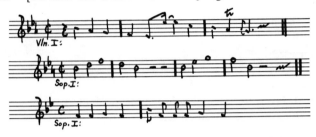

SSAB;Str.-E-Flat maj;G min;B-Flat maj.-*Lento. con Sordini;*
Munter. ohne Sordinen; Langsamer. con Sordini.-78m.
For an SS;Str. setting of first section, see Herbst 24.5.
For different settings of last section, see Herbst 13.7: *Herr ich*
warte...; Herbst 37.3: *Ave o du blass;* Herbst 42.9: *Er wird*
bey Ihnen wohnen; and Herbst 48.3: *Wer mich liebet.*

14.13   [Ich will ihnen wie ein Thau seyn—Wir freuen uns]

SS;Str/SSAB;Str.-F maj;B-Flat maj.-*Affettuoso. Nicht geschwinde;*
Munter, doch nicht zu geschwinde.-60m.-Hosea 6:4; 14:6; Jesaia 45:8;
Sacharja 2:10; Hohelied 2:16; Hosea 6:3.
A,B pts. for first section added in red ink.
For another version of *Wir freuen uns,* see Herbst 19.2.

14.14   [Mein Freund ist mein]

SSAB;Str.-F maj.-*Affettuoso.*-34m.-Hohelied 2:16.
For an adaptation by Gregor and Geisler, see Herbst 127.4.
Alternate text: *Was sehet....*

14.15   [Die Gnade unsers Herrn]

SSAB;Str.-F maj.-*Langsam.*-14m.-II.Corinther 13:13.
"So vollstimmig von Sängern als mogl. zu besezen."

15   GREGOR, CHRISTIAN (1723-1801) *Zum Kinder-Gemeintage am 23. May 1761*

15.1   [Ich habe euch noch viel]

SSAB;Str.-B-Flat maj.-*Mässig munter.*-42m.-Johannis 16:12,13.
At end: *"Choral: Drum bleiben wir."*

15.2   [Derselbige wird mich]

SSAB;Str.-E-Flat maj.-*Im vorigen Tempo.*-35m.-Johannis 16:14.
At end: *"Choral: 1.Drum bin ich; 2.Und seine ganze Busse; 3.Er weiss, was grosse Güther."*

15.3   [Meinen Frieden hinterlass ich euch]

SSAB;Str.-E-Flat maj.-*Langsam. con Sordini.*-32m.-Johannis 14:27.
At end: *"Choral: 1. Mit deinen heiligen Testamenten; 2. Und um der heiligen 5 Wunden."*

15.4   [Euer Herz erschrecke nicht]

SSAB;Str.-B-Flat min.-*Lebhaft. "die 4tel wie geschwinde 8tel."*-22m.-

Johannis 14:27,28.
At end: *"Choral: 1. Was Freude wird man; 2. Wenn du kommen wirst."*

15.5 [Es ist euch gut]

SSAB;Str.-B-Flat maj.-*im vorherigen Tempo.*-10m.-Johannis 16:7.
At end: *"Choral: Er liess sich in dem Heilgen; Mel. Te Deum"*

16 GREGOR, CHRISTIAN (1723-1801) *Zum Knäbgen Fest am 24. Juny 1761*

16.1 [Kommt her, ihr Kinder]

SS;Str.-B-Flat maj.-*Moderato.*-26m.-Psalm 34:12.
At end: *"Gem: Liebster Jesu wir sind hier"* [Hymn 3; Tune 84]

16.2 [So spricht der Herr: Siehe es kommt die Zeit]

SS;Str.-E-Flat maj.-*Munter.*-31m.-Ebräer 8:8.
At end: *"Choral: Wenn liebest du Sünder."*

16.3 [Das ist das neue Testament]

SSAB;cont.-E-Flat maj.-*Choral-Mensur.*-15m.-Ebräer 8:10.
"Ohne Instrumente; blos mit der Orgel."
Alternate text: *Dis ist der neue Bund.*
For another version, see Herbst 280.1.
At end: *"Gemeine: Den tiefen Eindruck"* [Hymn 821; Tune 14]

16.4   [Ich will ihr Gott seyn]

SSAB;Str. F min. *Etwas lebhafter, als voriges, die halben Noten, wie
geschwinde 4tel.-21m.-* Ebräer 8:10.
Alternate text: *Er will euer Gott seyn.*
For another version, see Herbst 280.1.
At end: *"Choral: Dankt Ihm mit Mund"* [Hymn 444; Tune 244].

16.5   [Es soll niemand seinen Nächsten]

SS;Str.-A-Flat maj;B-Flat maj.-*Munter.*-13m.-Ebräer 8:11.
At end: *"Choral: Ich muss Jesum selber."*

16.6   [Denn sie sollen mich]

SSAB;Str.-E-Flat maj.-*Andante.*-26m.-Ebräer 8:11.
At end: *"Choral: Der Freund der alten Sünder."*

16.7   [Und alle deine Kinder]

SS;Str.-B-Flat maj.-*Lebhaft.*.-19m.-Jesaia 54:13.
For another version, see Herbst 280.1 and Herbst 27.5.
At end: *"Choral: Wir sind in einer glükselgen Schul,
No. 1342. im Kl. Brr. Gesb."*

16.8   [Und grossen Frieden]

SSAB;Str.-B-Flat maj.-*Langsam.*-15m.-Jesaia 54:13.

For another version, see Herbst 280.1.
At end: *"Schluss: Der Kirchen-Segen."*

17 GREGOR, CHRISTIAN (1723-1801) *Zum Kinder Gemeintag am 25. July 1761*

17.1 *"Du Hirte Israel höre"*
Not in ms. See Herbst 13.3.
At end: *"Choral: Erschein uns in dem Bilde."*

17.2 [Ich bin der gute Hirte]

SSAB;Str.-D maj.-*Lebhaft, doch nicht zu geschwinde, sondern wie Andante.*-56m.-Johannis 10:12,3.
At end: *"Choral: Hier komm ich, mein Hirte! No. 1925 im Kl. Brr. Gesb."*

17.3 [Der Herr dein Gott wird dich lieben]

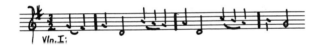

SSAB;Str.-G maj.-*Langsam.*-55m.-V.Mose 7:13
Losung for July 25, 1761.
At end: *"Choral Melod. In dulci jubilo ex G. dass du deine Kinder Ihm alle wieverliebst."*

17.4 *"Seine Kinder werden Ihm geboren...vid. Mus. zum 17. Aug. 1760"*
Not in ms. See Herbst 10.3: *Deine Kinder...*
At end: *"Choral: Das sind wie arme Kindelein."*

18 GREGOR, CHRISTIAN (1723-1801) *Zum 17. Aug. 1761*

18.1 [Wir warten deiner Güte]

SSAB;Str.-F maj.-*Andante.*-59m.-Psalm 48:10.
At end: *"Choral: Wie die Magdalene woll'n wir dich küssen"*

18.2   [Es freue sich]

SSAB;Str.-F maj.-*Etwas Munter.*-29m.-Psalm 48:12.
At end: *"Choral: Die Kirche ist ein Haus."*

18.3   [Der Herr richtet unsre Herzen]

SS;Str.-B-Flat maj.-*Langsam.*-57m.-II.Thessalonicher 3:5.
At end: *"Choral: Ach was du Herr."*

18.4   [Ich habe euch lieb—Und mein Vater]

SS;Str/SSAB;Str.-*Allegretto con Sordini; Andante in voriger Bewegung.*-
A maj.-66m;17m.-Matthäi 19:14; Johannis 14:23.
Losung der Kinder-Gemeine for August 17, 1761.
At end: *"Choral: Das macht uns Liebes-Schmerzen."* [Hymn 575,5]

18.5   [Lobe den Herrn meine Seele]

SSAB;Str.-A maj.-*Munter.*-50m.-Psalm 103:2.
See Herbst 22.1; Herbst [469.1].

At end: *"Choral: 1. O Wunder ohne Maassen* [Hymn 135,2];
2. Auff die dis jährge Mühe."

18.6   [Darum, dass seine Seele]

SS;Str.-D maj.-*Sehr langsam.*-56m.-Jesaia 53:11,12.
For an SSAB/SSAB vocal score, see Herbst 18.6b.
At end: *"Choral: Wo nicht eine Seele war."*

18.7   [Siehe wie gerne sie hingehn]

SSAB;Str.-G min.-*Lebhaft.*-36m.-Psalm 42:5.
At end: *"Choral: 1. Ja da fey'rt man; 2. Und heute tönte Ihm."*

18.8   [Das ist ein köstlich Ding]

SSTB;Str.-F maj.-*Andante.*-42m.Psalm 92:2.
At end: *"Choral: 1. Hallelujah, Lob Preis u. Macht* [Hymn 258,2];
2. Droben loben die in Frieden."

19   GREGOR, CHRISTIAN (1723-1801) *Zum 17. Aug. 1762*

19.1   [Siehe; alle Seelen sind mein—Ich will meinen Geist]

S recit.,arioso;fig.bass.-E-Flat maj.-[no tempo marking];
Lebhaft.-19m.-Ezechiel 18:4; Jesaia 45:11;
Ezechiel 36:27; 37:9; 35:15; 17:24.

19.2 [Ich gedenke noch wohl–Träufelt ihr Himmel–Wir freuen uns]

S recit;arioso/SS duet;fig.bass/SSAB;Organ(fig.bass).-E-Flat maj;D min.-[no tempo marking] ;*Munter;Vivace.*-84m. See Herbst 14.13.

19.3 [Gottes Brünnlein hat Wassers]

SSAB;cont.-C maj.-*Munter.*-25m.-Psalm 65:10.

19.4 [Ey! wie hat Er–Kommt her Kinder–Lasset die Kindlein–Und Er herzete sie]

S recit/arioso/SS duet/SSAB;cont.-G maj;C maj.-101m.-
V.Mose 33:3; Psalms 2:12; 45:3; Hohelied 5:15; Psalms 46:9; 34:9;
Matthäi 19:13,14,15.
For another version of *Kommt her...*, see Herbst 61.1.
Lasset die Kindlein: Losung der Kinder Gemeine for August 17, 1762.

19.5   [Herr unser Gott, du bist nocheben]

SSAB;cont.-A maj.-*Lebhaft.*-76m.-Psalm 4:7; Hohelied 1:2; 2:14;
Psalm 90:14.

19.6   [So spricht der Herr: Ich werde sie]

S recit;arioso;cont.-G maj.-47m.-II.Corinther 6:16; Jesaia 60:22.

19.7   [Was sollen wir mehr—Du bist der gute Hirte]

SSAB;cont.-D maj.-*Moderato;Ein wenig langsamer.*-77m.-
Johannis 10:12,3; Psalm 23:2,3.

20   GEISLER, JOHANN CHRISTIAN (1729-1815) *Zum 13. Januar. 1763*

20.1   [Gott, du hast dir ein Volk zubereitet]

SSAB;Str.-D maj;B min.-*Allegro.*49m.-II.Samuelis 7:24; Psalm 68:11
At end: quotation from Tune 151A (4-pt. harmonization).

20.2   [Du hast uns Brod vom Himmel gegeben]

SSAB;2Fl;Str.-D maj.-*Molto Andante.*-58m.- Johannis 6:31; Psalm 22:27.

21   GREGOR, CHRISTIAN (1723-1801) *Zum 2. Febr. 1763*

21.1   [Gott man lobet dich]

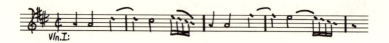

SSAB;Fl;Bn;Str.-D maj.-*Moderato.*-70m.-Psalm 65:2.

21.2   [Siehe, du hast Lust zur Wahrheit]

SSAB;Fl;Bn;Str.-B min.-*Etwas langsam.*-58m.-Psalm 51:8; Hymn 901,7
(Gerhard); Tune 151A.
For another version, see Herbst 26.1: *Ach Schönster unter allen.*
Adapted from J. P. Kellner's organ prelude.
Losung and Hymn for February 2, 1763.

22   GREGOR, CHRISTIAN (1723-1801) *Zum Friedensfest im
        H*[errn]*huth d. 21. Mart. 1763*

22.1   [Lobe den Herrn meine Seele]

SSAB;[2Fl;2Trpt];Str.-B-Flat maj.-*Moderat,Lebhaft.*-71m.-
Psalm 103.2.
Fl. and Trpt. pts. on separate sheets.
See Herbst 18.5; Herbst [469.1].

22.2   [Herr, Herr Gott! barmherzig]

SSAB;Str.-C min.-*Grave.*-39m.-II.Mose 34:6,7,; Psalm 40:6.
"Vide 2. Febr. 1765" [Herbst 54.1].
See Herbst 27.2; Herbst 54.1

22.3   [Ehre sey Gott in der Höhe]

SSAB;[2Fl;2Trpt] ;Str.-D maj.-*Moderato.*-56m.-Lucä 2:14.
Fl. and Trpt. pts. on separate sheets.
See Herbst 13.10 and 97.11.

22.4   [Gelobet sey der Herr! denn Er—Das ist ein Tag]

SSAB;[2Fl;2Trpt] ;Str.-B-Flat maj.-*Mässig,Lebhaft;Muntrer.*-
72m.-Psalms 28:6,7; 118:24; 95:2.
Fl. and Trpt. pts. on separate sheets.
For another version of *Das ist ein Tag,* see Herbst 100.1.
See Herbst 136.2.

22.5   [Aus dem Munde der jungen Kinder]

SSAB;cont.-B-Flat maj.-26m.-Psalms 8:3; 145:4.
"Die Instrumente gehen unisono mit den Singstimmen."

22.6   [Herr, unser Hort]

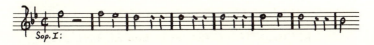

SSAB;Str.-B-Flat maj.-21m.-Psalm 27:5.

22.7   [Da schauen sie]

SSAB;Str.-B-Flat maj.-23m.-Psalm 46:9,10,11.

22.8   [Unser Herz freuet sich]

SSAB;[2Fl;Bn] ;Str.-B-Flat maj.-*Andante.*-82m.-Psalm 13:6;
Jesaia 63:1; Psalm 68:20.
Fl. and Bn. pts. on separate sheets.

22.9   [Dass die Stadt Gottes]

SSAB;[2Fl;Bn;2Hn] ;Str.-E-Flat maj.-*Nicht zu geschwinde.*-59m.-
Psalm 46:5,6.
Fl.,Bn.,Hn. pts. on separate sheets.

22.10   [Wünschet Jerusalem Glück]

SSAB;[2Fl;2Trpt] ;Str.-B-Flat maj.-*Andante.*-34m.-Psalm 122:6,7.
Fl. and Trpt. pts. on separate sheet.

22.11   [Dass in unserm Lande]

SSAB;Str.-G min.-*Lebhaft.*-59m.-Psalms 85:10-13; 145:16.

23   GREGOR, CHRISTIAN (1723-1801) *Zum 25. Mart. 1763*

23.1   [Wir haben ein Fest des Herrn]

SSAB.-B-Flat maj.-*Mässig, Lebhaft.*-47m.-II.Mose 10:9; Lucä 1:47;
Jeremia 23:23; Hosea 6:6; II Samuelis 22:10.

23.2   [Gross sind die Werke]

SSAB;cont.-*C maj.*-*Grave.*-36m.-Psalms 111:2; 66:8.
For same music, different text, see Herbst 23.3: *Meine Seele
erhebe den Herrn.*
Adapted from K. H. Graun's *Te Deum Laudamus,* no. 1 [See B VI].

23.3   [Meine Seele erhebe den Herrn]

SSAB;cont.-*C maj.*-*Grave.*-32m.-Luke 1:46-49.
For same music, different text, see Herbst 23.2: *Gross sind
die Werke des Herrn.*
Adapted from K. H. Graun's *Te Deum Laudamus,* no. 1 [See B VI].

24   GREGOR, CHRISTIAN (1723-1801) *Zum gr. Sabbath 1763*

24.1   [Mein Herz dichtet ein feines Lied]

S;[Fl] ;Str.-*G maj.*-*Langsam.*-14m.-Psalm 45:2.
Flute pt. on separate sheet.

24.2   [Herr, ich will deinem Namen]

S;[Fl] ;Str.-*E-Flat maj.*-*Andante.*-87m.-Psalms 30:5; 57:8; 145:5; 71:8.
Flute pt. on separate sheet.
Alternate text: *Gott, ich will dir ein neues Lied singen.*

24.3   [Gelobet sey der Herr, gross von Rath]

SSAB; cont.-B-Flat maj; E-Flat maj.-60m.-Jeremia 32:19; Psalm 111:4;
Ebräer 9:16.

24.4   [Fürwahr, Er trug unsre Krankheit]

SSAB;cont.-E-Flat maj.-*Langsam und sanft.*-45m.-Jesaia 53:4-6.

24.5   [Da sind wir worden]

SS;Str.-E-Flat maj.-*Angenehm u. langsam. con Sordini.*-75m.-Hohelied
8:10; 1:2,3; Psalm 45:9; Jesaia 53:3; Psalm 45:3.
See Herbst 14.12.

24.6   [Und da alles vollendet war]

SSAB;[Fl] ;Str.-A min.-*Andante.*-68m.-Johannis 19:30; II.
Mose 31:17; 16:23; Jesaia 11:10.
Flute pt. on separate sheet.

24.7   [Unbeschreiblich schöner]

S;Str.-E-Flat maj.-*Andantino. con Sordini.*-77m.-Hymn 576,
var. (Zinzendorf).

24.8 [Nun ruht Er]

SSAB;[Fl] ;Str.-B min.-*Moderato. con Sordini.*-50m.-II.Mose 31:17; 16:23;
Jesaia 11:10.
Flute part on separate sheet.

25 GREGOR, CHRISTIAN (1723-1801) *Zum 4. May 1763*

25.1 [Der Herr hat grosses—Freuet euch und seyd fröhlich]

SSAB;[2Fl] ;Str.-B-Flat maj.-*Moderato; Affettuoso.*-89m.-
Psalms 126:3; 16:7; 36:8; 69:33; 71:17.
Flute pts.on separate sheet.
See Herbst 80.5.

25.2 [Gross ist der Herr]

SS;Str.-B-Flat maj.-*Moderato.*-55m.-Psalm 48:2; Hymn.
Losung and Hymn for May 4, 1763.

25.3 [Wohl dem Volke, dess der Herr]

SSAB;[Str] ;cont.-E-Flat maj.-*Lebhaft.*-67m.-Psalm 33:12; I.Königen 9:3;
Hosea 2:19; Psalms 40:5; 48:15; 36:11; 34:19; 21:7.
*"Nota: Wenn die Instrumente weg bleiben so bleibt auch das
Praeludium u. der Schluss weg."*

25.4   [Küsse uns, wenns Herz]

SS;Str.-C min.-*Affettuoso, con Sordini.*-97m.-Hymn 839,5 (Zinzendorf).
See Herbst 35.1.

25.5   [Es bleibt dabey]

SB;Str.-G min.-*Mässig lebhaft.*-60m.-Hymn.

26   GREGOR, CHRISTIAN (1723-1801) *Zum Gr. Agnes Geburts-tag am 14. May 1763*

26.1   [Ach Schönster unter allen]

SS;Str.-C min.-*Adagio.*-80m.-Hymn 647,2 (C. R. von Zinzendorf);
Tune 151A.
For another version, see Herbst 21.2: *Siehe, du hast Lust zur Wahrheit.*

26.2   [Du bist unsre Zuversicht]

SS;Str.-E-Flat maj.-*Arienmässig con Sordini.*-136m.-Psalms 46:2;
71:23; Hymn.
Losung and Hymn for May 14, 1763.

26.3   [Du allerschönster]

SS;Str.-A-Flat maj.-*Affettuoso u. Langsam.*-62m.-Hymn 209 (Gregor).

27   GREGOR, CHRISTIAN (1723-1801) *Zum Feste der Knäblein am 24. Juny 1763*

27.1   [Gelobet sey der Herr, der Gott Israel]

SSB;2Fl;2Trpt(or Hn);Str;Fondamento.-D maj.-*Moderat Lebhaft.*-62m.-Lucä 1:68-75.

27.2   [Herr, Herr Gott! barmherzig]

SSB;Str.-B min.-*Langsam;jedoch lebhaft.*-32m.-II. Mose 34:6; Jesaia 57:15; Johannis 1:14.
See Herbst 22.2 and 54.1.

27.3   [Nun, das Kindlein]

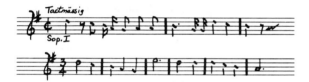

S/SSB;Str;cont.-G maj.-*Munter.*-53m.-Lucä 1:80,76,77; Jesaia 40:3-5.

27.4   [O Herr, du ewiger Gott]

SSB;Str.-E min.-*Lebhaft.*-61m.-Jesaia 40:28-31; Lucä 7:28; Ebräer 2:14;
Johannis 17:19.

27.5   [Denn sie sollen dich—Und alle deine Kinder]

SSB;Str.-E-Flat maj.-incomplete.
"Denn sie sollen...vide die Fest Mus. vom 24. Juny 1761, No. 6.
[Herbst 16.6] *dasselbst, u. NB folgendes gleich dran gehangen."*
See Herbst 16.7 and 280.1.

27.6   [Nun der Gott des Friedens]

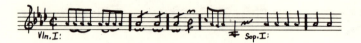

SSB;Str.-A-Flat maj.-*Lebhaft. con Sordini.*-95m.-I.Thessalonicher 5:23.
Text for June 24, 1763.

28   GREGOR, CHRISTIAN (1723-1801) *Zur Einweyhung des Flügels
am led. Brr. Hause Herrnhuth am 14. Aug. 1763*
[Siehe, wie fein und lieblich]
Duetto

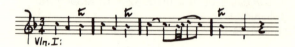

SS;2Fl;2Hn;Str;Fondamento.-F maj.-*Affettuoso.*-79m.-Psalm 133:1,3.
At end: *"Choral: Du süsse Liebe"* [Hymn 297,3].

29   GREGOR, CHRISTIAN (1723-1801) *Zum 17. Aug. 1763*

29.1   [Heiliger Herre Gott!]

SSAB;cont.-F maj.-*Langsam.*-96m.-Hymn 1464(Litany); Tune 519;
Psalms 40:6; 8:5; I.Johannis 4:19; 3:16; Offenbarung 5:9; Psalm 31:6;
Klaglieder 3:22,23; Jesaia 38:17; Psalms 65:12; 111:9; 102:19.
See Herbst 7.4

29.2   [Wie solln wir]

SS[T]B;Str.-F maj.-*Langsam. con Sordini.*-45m.-Psalm 116:12;
I.Mose 32:10.
Tenor pt. added in red ink.
See Herbst [469.2]

29.3 [Gib mir, mein Kind, dein Herz]

S;Str.-G min.-*Moderato.*-29m.-Hymn 406,1.

29.4 [Es sollen wol Berge—Danket dem Herrn]
Chorus.

SSAB;cont.-B-Flat maj.-98m.-Jesaia 54:10; Psalm 136:1;
Apostelgeschichte 17:27; Klaglieder 3:25; Matthäi 18:11; Lucä 15:5;
Johannis 6:37.
See Herbst 8.3.

29.5 [Hier komm ich]

SSA[T]B;Str.-E-Flat maj.-*Affettuoso.*-123m.-Hymn 700,3.
Tenor pt.added in red ink.

29.6 [Unser Herr Jesus Christus]

SS/SSAB;Str.-F maj.-*Langsam.*-131m.-I.Petri 1:7,8; Galater 3:1;
Epheser 5:19.

30 GREGOR, CHRISTIAN (1723-1801) *Zum Ehe-Chor-Fest am
7. Septembr. 1763*

30.1a   [Du hast durch deine Schöpfers]

S;Str.-E-Flat maj.-*Lebhaft u. gestossen.*-39m.-Hymn 290,5,var; Tune 22B.
Chorale with str.acc.
For another version, see Herbst 135.3.
See also Herbst 55.1.

30.1b   [Gott der Herr]

T;Str.-E-Flat maj.-*Bedächtiger.*-25m.-I.Mose 2:7,21,22.

30.2   [Der Die Braut hat]

SSAB;Str.-G maj.-*Andante.*-56m.-Johannis 3:29; Jesaia 54:5; Hosea 2:19;
I.Thessalonicher 5:10; Apostelgeschichte 20:28; Epheser 5:32.

30.3   [Herr unser Gott, du bist nocheben]

SS/SSAB;cont.-G maj.-88m.-Matthäi 19:4; 18:20; Jeremia 14:20;
Klaglieder 3:57; Jacobi 1:5; Psalm 4:7; Jesaia 33:2; Psalm 51:10;
Hohelied 1:2; Jesaia 49:2; Psalm 90:14.
"Ohne Instrumente, u. ohne sich an den Tact zu binden."

30.4   [Wie fein sind deine Hütten]

SSAB;Str.-G maj.-*Andante.*-80m.-IV.Mose 24:5; Jeremia 30:19,
Psalm 147:1.
See Herbst 65.3

30.5   [Singet um einander]

SS/SSAB;Str.-B-Flat maj.-*Andante u. gestossen.*-97m.-Psalm 147:7,1;
V.Mose 26:3; I.Könige 8:15; Psalms 143:5; 77:12; 119:105; 32:8; 61:8;
115:14.

30.6   [Der Weiber Schmuck]

SS/SSAB;Str.-E-Flat maj.-*Andante,con Sordini.*-114m.-I.Petri 3:3,4;
Jesaia 61:10; Matthäi 23:37.

30.7   [Was sollen wir mehr—Du Liebhaber]

SSAB;Str.-F maj.-*Langsam;Etwas munterer.*-132m.-Hiob 7:20;
I.Mose 32:10; Psalms 106:5; 23:6.

31   [UNIDENTIFIED] *Am 22. Nov. 1763*
missing

32   GREGOR, CHRISTIAN (1723-1801) *Zur Christ-Nacht am 24 Dec. 1763.*

32.1   [Mein Herz dichtet ein feines Lied]

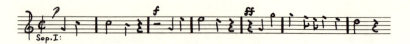

SSAB.-C maj.-*Langsam.*-15m.-Psalm 45:2.
See Herbst 37.1.

32.2   [Mein Herz ist bereit—Ja singet alle]

SSAB.-D maj.-*Lebhaft;Munterer.*-36m.-Psalm 57:8; Hymn.
See Herbst 37.2, 64.1, and 91.1.

32.3   [Der Berg Zion]

SSAB.-E-Flat maj.-*Munter.*-18m.
Losung for December 24, 1763.

32.4   [Ja Christnacht]

SSAB.-C maj.-*Munter.*-34m.-Hymn 85(Gregor).
See Herbst 32.2, 37.2, 64.1, and 91.1.

33.1   GREGOR, CHRISTIAN (1723-1801) *Text vom 28 Dec. 1763*
        [Gnade sey mit allen]

SSAB;cont.-D maj.-49m.-Epheser 6:24.

At end: *"Choral. Bleibet ewig sitzen an den Wundenritzen"* [Hymn 1059,3].

33.2   ?GREGOR, CHRISTIAN (1723-1801) *Text zum 29 Dec. 1763* [Der Herr des Friedens]

SSAB;cont.-F maj.-37m.-II.Thessalonicher 3:16.
At end: *"Choral. Und siegle uns der Sünde nu."*

33.3   ?GREGOR, CHRISTIAN (1723-1801) *Text zum 30. Dec.* [1763] [Der Friede Gottes der höher ist]

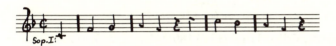

SSAB;cont.-F maj.-36m.-Philipper 4:7.
At end: *"Choral. Christe du Lamm Gottes"* [Hymn 103,3].

34   GREGOR, CHRISTIAN (1723-1801) *Zur Nacht-Wache am 31. December 1763.*

34.1   [Der Herr ist mein Hirte]

SSAB.-E-Flat maj.-*Munter u. Zufrieden.* 20m.-Psalm 23:1.
Losung for December 28, 1763.
At end: *"Choral. Zur Stärke u. zur Nahrung."*

34.2   [Du Herr allein hilfest mir]

SSAB.-E-Flat maj.-*Langsam, doch nicht zu sehr.*-20m.-Psalm 4:9.
Losung for December 29, 1763.
At end: *"Choral. Weil das Täublein"* [Kl.Br.Ges: Hymn 2395,10].

34.3   [Deine Güte ist vor meinen Augen]

SSAB.-C min.-*Moderat Munter.*-16m.-Psalm 26:3.
Losung for December 30, 1763.
At end: *"Choral. So gehn wir in Zerflossenheit."*

34.4   [Der Herr ist meine Stärke]

SSAB.-*Lebhaft, doch nicht geschwinde.*-21m.-Psalm 28:7.
Losung for December 31, 1763.
At end: *"Dem Lamm das geschlachtet ist"*

35   GREGOR, CHRISTIAN (1723-1801) *Zum 2. Febr. 1764*

35.1   [Küsse uns, wenns Herz]

SSAB.-A min.-*Langsam.*-28m.-Hymn 839,5(Zinzendorf).
For another arr., see Herbst 25.4.

35.2   [Guter Freund]

SSAB.-A maj.-*Langsam.*-31m.-Hymn 2008,6 [Kl.Brr.Ges.].

36   [UNIDENTIFIED] *Zur Gedächtniss-Predigt Chur-Fürst Friedrich
Christians zu Sachsen am 6. Febr. 1764*

36.1   [Herr Gott Zebaoth!]

SSAB.-E-Flat maj.-*Lebhaft.*-19m.-Psalm 80:4,5.
At end: *"Choral: Erschein uns in dem Bilde."*

36.2   [Meine Augen sehnen sich]

SSAB.-F min.-*Langsam.*-18m.-Psalm 119:82.
At end: *"Choral: Die ganze Welt erfreuet mich nicht."*

36.3   [Der Herr verstösset nicht ewiglich]

SSAB.-B-Flat maj.-*Lebhaft.*-14m.-Klaglieder 3:31-33.
At end: *"Choral: Sein Herz ist weich."*

36.4   [Wenn ich mitten in der Angst]

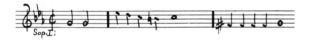

SSAB.-C min.-*Nicht zu langsam.*-13m.-Psalm 138:7.
At end: *"Choral: Deine Pein und blütigs Schweizen."*

36.5   [Wenn ich im Finstern sitze]

SSAB.-F maj.-*Nicht zu langsam.*-10m.-Micha 7:8.
At end: *"Choral: Gibts gleich nicht"* [Hymn 1027,4].

36.6   [Solches geschiehet auch vom Herrn]

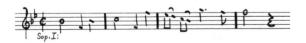

SSAB.-B-Flat Maj.-*Mässig munter.*-17m.-Jesaia 28:29.
At end: *"Choral: Drum lass ich Ihn."*

36.7   [Unsre Seele harret] *"Vide Music zum 4. May 1764"* [Herbst 38.5]
"Choral: Alles Ding währt seine Zeit."

36.8   [Ich will schweigen]

SSAB.-C min.-*Lebhaft.*-23m.-Psalm 39:10.
At end: *"Choral: Gedenk'n will ich."*

37   GREGOR, CHRISTIAN (1723-1801) *Zum grossen Sabbath Ao. 1764*

37.1   [Mein Herz dichtet ein feines Lied]

SSAB;Str.-C maj.-*Andante.*-45m.-Psalm 45:2.
See Herbst 32.1.

37.2   [Lasset uns—Mein Herz ist bereit—Ja singet alle—Ich will dem Herrn
        singen—Mein Mund hat sich—Herr, wenn du auszogst—Und da du
        in Gethsemane]

SS/SSAB/SSAB/SS/SSAB/SSAB/S;Str.-G maj;C maj;F maj;D min;
B-Flat maj; G min.-*Lebhaft wie 2/4 Takt;Munter;Moderater;
Andante.*-148m.-II.Mose 15:21; Psalm 57:8; Hymn; Richter 5:3,4;
I.Samuelis 2:1,2; Hymn.
See Herbst 32.2, 64.1, and 91.1.

37.3   [Ave o du blass und bleiche]

SSAB;Str.-C maj.-*Langsam, con Sordini sempre piano*-17m.-Hymn 160,1
(C.R.von Zinzendorf).
For alternate texts, see Herbst 13.7: *Herr ich warte auf dein Heil;*
Herbst 14.12: *Und Sein Name;* Herbst 42.9: *Er wird bey Ihnen wohnen;*
Herbst 48.3: *Wer mich liebet.*

38   GREGOR, CHRISTIAN (1723-1801) *Zum 4. May 1764*

38.1   [Singet dem Herrn alle Lande]

SSAB;[2Trpt];Str.-D maj.-*Lebhaft.*-168m.-I.Chronica 17:23,28,25,29,27;
Psalm 135:3; I.Chronica 17:34; Jesaia 61:3; Psalms 147:3; 149:4.
Losung for May 4, 1764.
Trpt.pts.on separate sheet.
For a variant version, see Herbst 66.1.

38.2   [Wie sind wir doch]

S;[2Hns];Str.-G maj.-*Lebhaft.*-46m.-Hymn 754,8 (Zinzendorf); Tune 228.
Hn.pts.on separate sheet.
*"Kann auch 3. oder 4. stimmig gesungen werden. das ganze Stück
kan auch ins F transponirt werden."*

38.3   [Den tiefen Eindruck]

SSAB.-E min.-*Langsam. Ohne Instrumente.*-39m.-Hymn 821,1
(C.R.von Zinzendorf).

38.4   [Ich umfange Herz]

S;Str.-B-Flat maj.-*Andante.*-28m.-Hymn 132:2,1; Tune 165A.

38.5   [Unsre Seele harret]

SSAB;cont.-E-Flat maj.-49m.-Psalm 33:20-22.
"Ohne Instrumente."

38.6   [Habe deine Lust]

SSAB;Str.-G maj.-*Andante.*-107m.-Psalm 37:4.

39   GEISLER, JOHANN CHRISTIAN (1729-1815) *Zum 24. Juny 1764*

39.1   [Lobe den Herrn meine Seele, und was in mir]

SS;Str.-A maj.-*Munter.*-72m.-Psalm 103:1-5.

39.2   [Barmherzig und gnädig ist der Herr]

SSAB.-14m.-Psalm 103:8,10,11.

39.3   [Wie sich ein Vater über Kinder erbarmet]
        Duetto.

SS;Str.-D maj.-87m.-Psalm 103:13,14.

39.4 [Die Gnade des Herrn]

SS;Str.-D maj.-*Munter.*-22m.-Psalm 103:17,18.
Incomplete. At end: *"Drum singet alle meine glieder.*
Vid. Mus. zum gr. Sabbath 1764 di Gregor" [Herbst 37.2].

40 GEISLER, JOHANN CHRISTIAN (1729-1815) *Zum Kinder-Gemeintag*
am 14. July 1764
missing

41 GREGOR, CHRISTIAN (1723-1801) *Losung am 29. Aug. 1764*
di Gregor
[Er ist Joseph]

B/SSAB;Str.-D maj.-*Etwas Munter.*-75m.-I.Mose 45:4,5.
Text substitutions added in red ink: *Er ist Jesus.*
See Herbst 286b.

42 GEISLER, JOHANN CHRISTIAN (1729-1815) *Zum 29. Aug. 1764*
di Geisler

42.1 [Singet dem Herrn ein neues Lied und lobet]

SSAB;Str.-D maj.-48m.-Psalms 96:1,2; 100:2,3.
For another version, see Herbst 118.1. See also Herbst 92.

42.2 [Herr mein Gott! du hilfst den Elenden]

SSAB;Str.-B min;A maj.-*Grave.*-36m.-Psalms 149:4; 147:3.

42.3   [Du Heiliger in Israel]
       Aus dem Graunschen Te Deum.

SSAB.-D maj.-56m;*"Idem alio modo."*46m.-Psalms 71:22; 104:1.
Paraphrase of Graun's *Te Deum Laudamus*, no.4. [see BVI]

42.4   [Unsre Augen werden den König sehen]

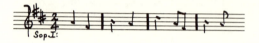

SSTT;2Fl;Str;Org.-D maj;A maj.-50m.-Jesaia 33:17; Hohelied 5:10;
Psalm 45:3.
"Fl. Trav./Oder mit einem 4 füssen Flöten Register auf der Orgel."

42.5   [Wie die Kinder Fleisch und Blut haben]

SS;cont.-A maj.-16m.-Ebräer 2:14; I.Mose 45:4.

42.6   [Wir freuen uns und sind fröhlich]

SSTT/SSSB;Str.-A maj.-11m.

42.7   [Er musste allerdings Seinen Brüdern]

SS;cont.-A maj.-9m.-Ebräer 2:17.

42[.8]   [Er ist versucht worden]

SS;cont.-A maj;B min.-10m.-Ebräer 4:15; 2:18.
Unnumbered on ms., follows 42.7.

42.9   [Er wird bey Ihnen wohnen]

SSAB;Str.-D maj;A maj.-23m.-Offenbarung 21:3; 22:3,4.
For other versions of the last section, see Herbst 13.7: *Herr, ich warte...;*
Herbst 14.12: *Und Sein Name;* Herbst 37.3: *Ave o du blass...;* Herbst
48.3: *Wer mich liebet...*

42.10   [Nun Herr! segne dein Erbe]

SSAB;Str.-D maj.-*Münter.*-35m.-Psalms 28:9; 5:12; 103:4.

43   GREGOR, CHRISTIAN (1723-1801) and JOHANN CHRISTIAN
         GEISLER (1729-1815)
         *Die/Geschichte Josephs/I.Mos.37.42.43./nebst der/von der Gemeine
         gemachten Application/auf/unsern lieben Herrn, Freund u. Bruder bey
         einem L.M. in Marienborn d. 29. Aug. 1764/gesungen./di Gregor
         & Geisler.*

SB/SSAB;Str.-D maj.-336m.-I.Mose 37,42,43.
Chorales interspersed with solos and choruses.
Contains excerpts from Gregor's *Er ist Joseph.* [Herbst 41].

44   [UNIDENTIFIED] *Zum 1. October. 1764. In der Morgen Liturgie.*

44.1   [Sehet, welch eine Liebe]
Chorus.

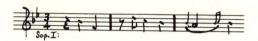

SSAB.-B-Flat maj.-27m.-I.Johannis 3:1.

44.2   [Gelobet sey Gott]

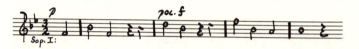

SSAB.-B-Flat maj.-42m,incomplete: *"Introitus zu Er will uns damit locken* [Herbst 44.3] *wenn solche mit diesem an einander gehangen wird."*-Epheser 1:3.
Text for October 1, 1764.

44.2b   [Gelobet sey Gott]

SSAB.-E-Flat maj.-58m.-Epheser 1:3.-*"Der vorhergehende Text, auf andre Weise, wenn ein Choral drauf folgt, ehe das kommt: Er will uns damit locken."*
Text for October 1, 1764.

44.3   [Er will uns damit locken] *Zum 8. Aug. 1764 in Marienborn.*

SSAB.-B-Flat maj.-*Andante.*-38m.

44.4   [Dank sey dem Vater] *Beym L*[iebes] *Mahl*

SSAB.-E-Flat maj.-38m.-Colosser 1:12,13; Epheser 1:5,6.

44.5   [Denn nichts ist zu melden]

SSAB.-E-Flat maj.-14m.-Hymn 1546,4-5 (Simon Graff); Tune 122.

44.6   [Dem, der überschwänglich]

SSAB.-B-Flat maj.-*Lebhaft; Gravitaetischer.*-22m.-Epheser 3:20,21.

45   GEISLER, JOHANN CHRISTIAN (1729-1815) *Zum 1. Oct. 1764*
      [Welch ein Name! heiligt Ihn]

SSABB;Str.-G min.-15m.-Hymn.

46   GREGOR, CHRISTIAN (1723-1801) *Zum 13. Nov. 1764*

46.1   [Komm weide du dein Volk]

SSAB;Str.-A maj.-*Arienmässig u. etwas lebhaft.*-57m.-Micha 7:14.

46.2   [Siehe, Er kommt]

B;Str.-D maj.-*Tactmässig.*-16m.-Ezechiel 34:11,14,16.

46.3   [Wer sich rühmen will]

SSAB;[2Cl;2Hn] ; Str.-E-Flat maj.-*Moderato.*-75m.-Jeremia 9:24;
V.Mose 10:21; 32:43.
Cl. and Hn. pts. on separate sheets.

47   GEISLER, JOHANN CHRISTIAN (1729-1815) *Zum 13. Novembr. 1764*

47.1   [Lobet den Herrn euren Gott!]

SSAB;Str.-D maj.-55m.-Joel 2:26; Psalm 68:35; Jeremia 50:2;
Psalm 147:1.

47.2   [Unsre Seele soll sich rühmen]

SSAB;cont.-D maj.-19m.-incomplete: *"Vide Music zum 25. Mart.
1763 u. 64 in* H[errn]*huth."*-Psalm 34:3; Lucä 1:49.
Complete, with different text, in Herbst 23.3
Adapted from K. H. Graun's *Te Deum Laudamus*, no. 1 [See B VI].

47.3   [Israel freue sich]

SSAB;Str.-G maj.-46m.

48   GEISLER, JOHANN CHRISTIAN (1729-1815) *Zum Kinder-Gemein-
Tage am 1. Decembr. 1764*

48.1   [Unsre Seele ist stille]

SS;Str.-E-Flat maj.-*Mässig u. ruhig.*-65m.-Psalms 62:2; 145:18; 10:17.

48.2 [Siehe Er stehet vor der Thür]

SS;Str.-E-Flat maj.-*Molto Andante.*-58m.-Offenbarung 3:20.

48.3 [Seine Lust ist bey den Menschenkindern]

SS;Str.-E-Flat maj;B-Flat maj.-55m.-Sprüche 8:31; Marci 12:33; Johannis 14:23.
For other versions of the last section, see Herbst 13.7: *Herr, ich warte...*; Herbst 14.12: *Und Sein Name*; Herbst 37.3: *Ave o du blass...*; Herbst 42.9: *Er wird bey Ihnen wohnen.*

49 GEISLER, CHRISTIAN GOTTFRIED (1730-1810) *Die Geschichte der Geburt des Heilands Luc. 2. zum 24. Decembr: 1764*
[Es begab sich]

S recit;SS;Str.-G maj.-incomplete: *"Vide Christnachts Music 1760"*
[Herbst 13.10].
Gregor's *Ehre sey Gott* from Christmas music, 1760 inserted.

50a GREGOR, CHRISTIAN (1723-1801) *Zum Knaben-Fest am 13. Jan. 1765*
[Jesus nahm zu an Weisheit]

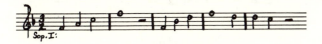

SSAB.-F maj.-*"Textus".*-28m.-Lucä 2:52.

50b   GREGOR, CHRISTIAN (1723-1801) *Zum Knaben-Fest am 12. Jan. 1766*
[Jesus nahm zu an Weisheit]

SSB;2Hns;Str.-F maj.-*Moderato.*-69m.-Lucä 2:52.
"*Vorstehender Text noch einmal 12. Jan. 1766*"

51   GEISLER, JOHANN CHRISTIAN (1729-1815) *Zum 13. Jan. 1765*
[Jesus nahm zu an Weisheit]

S;Str.-C maj.-*Moderato.*-28m.-Lucä 2:52.

52   HERBST, JOHANNES (1735-1812) *Bey Beerdigung der Schw. Augusta Erdmuth v. Tschirsky in Gnadenfrey am 15. Januar 1765*
[Schlaf liebes Kind]

SS;Str.-A min.-*Arietta con Sordini.*-46m.-Hymn 1724 (Zinzendorf); Tune 483
Added in different hand: "*Composto di* [Herbst] *Gnadenfrey.*"
Alternate text: *Schlaf lieber Bruder.*

53   GREGOR, CHRISTIAN (1723-1801) *Zum 26. Jan. 1765*

53.1   [Du sollt deinen Kindern]
Losung zum Kinder-Gemein-Tag am 26. Januar. 1765

SSAB;Str.-E-Flat maj.-*Affettuoso.*-77m.-V.Mose 4¾49.
For alternate text, see Herbst 53.2.
At end: "*Choral: Dass in dem Herzen immer seinen.*"

53.2   [Das ist die rechte Gnade]
        Text zum Kinder-Gemein-Tag am 26. Januar. 1765

SSAB;Str.-E-Flat maj.-77m.-I.Petri 5:12.
"Voriges mit dem Texte des Tages. die Instrument stimmen
bleiben unverändert."

53.2[b] GEISLER, JOHANN CHRISTIAN (1729-1815) *Zum Kinder-*
         Gemein-Tag, am 26. Jan. 1765
         [Das ist die rechte Gnade]

SS;Str.-B-Flat maj.-*Moderato.*-51m.-I.Petri 5:12.

54   GREGOR, CHRISTIAN (1723-1801) *Zum 2. Febr. 1765*

54.1   [So lass nun die Kraft—Herr, Herr Gott! barmherzig]

SB/SSAB;Str.-E-Flat maj.-*Largo;Adagio.*-93m.-IV.Mose 14:17.
Losung for Feb. 2, 1765.
For a slightly altered version, see Herbst 54.1[b].
See also Herbst 22.2 and 27.2

54.1[b] [So lass nun, Herr, deine Kraft—Herr, Herr Gott! barmherzig]

SB/SSAB;Str.-E-Flat maj.-*Larghetto;Adagio.*-98m.-IV.Mose 14:17.
Losung for February 2, 1765.
For a slightly altered version, see Herbst 54.1.
See also Herbst 22.2 and 27.2

54.2   [Unser Wandel ist im Himmel]

SB;Str.-A min.-*Larghetto.*-51m.-Philipper 3:20.

54.3   [Ich weiss an wen ich gläube]

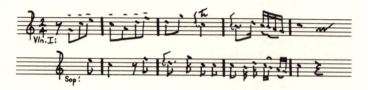

SB;Str.-C maj.-*Mässig,Lebhaft.*-71m.-II. Timotheum 1:12.

55   GREGOR, CHRISTIAN (1723-1801) *Zum 25. Mart. 1765*

55.1   [Also hat Gott die Welt]

SSTB;Str.-G maj.-*Vivace.*-39m.-Hymns 274,1(Zinzendorf),55,2; Tune 22B.
For alternate text, see Herbst 30.1 and 135.3: *Du hast durch deine
Schöpfers.*

55.2   [Kindlein bleibet bey ihm]

SSTB;Str.-G maj.-*Affettuoso u. nicht zu geschwind.*-106m.-I.Johannis
2:28; I. Corinther 6:20.

56   GEISLER, JOHANN CHRISTIAN (1729-1815) *d. 4. Apr. 1765.
di Geisler*
[Da kam Jesus mit ihnen]
Geschichte am grünen Donnerstage

S;Chorus;Congregation;Str.-*Largo, sempre piano.*-Matthäi 26:36-44;

Johannis 18:1,2; Lucä 22:41-44.
Recitatives, ariosos, interspersed with indications for chorales.

57   GEISLER, JOHANN CHRISTIAN (1729-1815) *Am Char-Freitag*
       d. 5. Apr. 1765
       Geschichte zum Charfreytage

S/SSAB;Str.-Jesaia 53:12; Matthäi 27:33,34,45-47; Lucä 23:33,34,39-46;
Johannis 19:25-28,30.
Recitatives, ariosos, choruses, chorales.
Contains paraphrased excerpts from Graun's *Der Tod Jesu.*

58   GEISLER, JOHANN CHRISTIAN (1729-1815) *Zum grossen Sabbath*
       d. 6. Apr. 1765

58[.1] [Es ist noch eine Ruhe]

SSAB;Str.-G min.-*Lento.*-29m.-Ebräer 4:9.
Text for April 6, 1765.

58[.2] [Wir wünschen uns zu aller Zeit]

S;Str.-E-Flat maj.-35m. Hymn 1110,4; Tune 22B with instr. obbligato.

59   GREGOR, CHRISTIAN (1723-1801) *Zum Ostertage 1765*
       [Halt in Gedächtniss]

SSAB;[2Trpt or Hn];Str.-D maj.-*Gravitaetisch.*-47m.-II.Timotheum 2:8;
Offenbarung 1:18.
Brass pts.on separate sheet.

60   GEISLER, JOHANN CHRISTIAN (1729-1815) *Zum Kinder-Gemein-*
       Tage d. 13. July, 1765 in Gnadenfrey

60.1   [Der Herr ist freundlich]

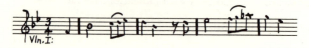

SS;Str.-B-Flat maj.-*Lebhaft.*-67m.-Klaglieder 3:25; Jesaia 38:17;
Offenbarung 5:9.

60.2   [Der Herr ist mein Theil]

SS;Str.-E-Flat maj.-*Lebhaft.*-51m.-Klaglieder 3:24; Hohelied 3:4.

61.1   GEISLER, JOHANN CHRISTIAN (1729-1815) *Zum 17. Aug. 1765*
        [Kommt her Kinder]

SS;Str.-B-flat maj.-*Moderato.*-59m, incomplete.
Ms.marked: *"No. 61 u. 62"*
See Herbst 19.4.

61.2   GREGOR, CHRISTIAN (1723-1801) *Zum 17. Aug. 1765*
        [Wenn schlägt die angenehme Stunde]

SS;Str.-E-Flat maj.-*Allegretto.*-incomplete.

61.3   [O dass Ihn doch]
        missing

[62]   ?GREGOR, CHRISTIAN (1723-1801)
        [Die Stätte unsers Heiligthums]
        Partitur zu einem Texte im led. Brr. Liede an ihrem Fest d. 29.
        Aug. 1765

SS;2Hns;Str.-E-Flat maj.-*Nicht zu geschwinde.*-85m.-Jeremia 17:12; Hymn.

63   GEISLER, JOHANN CHRISTIAN (1729-1815) *Zum 29. Aug. 1765.*
      in Gnadenfrey di Geisler

63.1   [Wir wollen der Güte des Herrn gedenken]

SSAB;2Hns;Str.-D maj.-123m.-Jesaia 63:7; Psalms 54:8; 92:2.

63.2   [Er hat sich unsrer Seelen]

SS;TT/SSAB;2Fl;Str;Clavicembalo.-G maj.-*Andante.*-80m.-Jesaia 38:17;
61:10.

63.3   [Der Herr hat uns]

SSAB;Str;Clavicembalo.-E maj.-32m.

63.4   [Gelobet, und haltet]

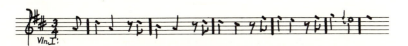

SSAB;2Hns;Str.-D maj.-43m.-Psalm 76:12; II.Timotheum 2:3.

63.5   [Der Herr ist unsre Kraft—Er hat uns heraus]

SSAB/TT;Vla;Vcl. obbl;Str/Clavicembalo.-A maj.-19m.-Habacuc 3:19;
I.Königen 8:57.

63.6   [Er wird sein Gesez]

SSAB;Str;Clavicembalo.-A maj.-40m.-Jeremia 31:33; Jesaia 55:3.

64   GREGOR, CHRISTIAN (1723-1801) *Zum 7. Sept. 1765*

64.1   [Mein Herz ist bereit—Ja singet alle]

SSAB;2Hns;Str.-B-Flat maj.-*Lebhaft;Muntrer.*-50m.-Psalm 57:8; Hymn.
See also Herbst 32.2, 37.2 and 91.1.

64.2   [Vor Ihm ist Freude]

SSAB;2Hns;Str.-F maj.-*Angenehm u. nicht zu geschwinde.*-34m.-
Psalm 16:11.
"V. Mus. z. 4. May 1761. No. 3. Vor dir ist Freude" [Herbst 14.3].

64.3   [Mein Freud der weiss]

SSAB;2Hns;Str.-F maj.-*Affettuoso.*-37m.-Hymn.
For alternate text, see Herbst 7.6: *Da sind wir arm.*

65   GEISLER, JOHANN CHRISTIAN (1729-1815) *Zum 7. Sept. 1765.
in Gnadenfrey*

65.1   [Ich will vor dem Herrn spielen]

SSAB;2Hns;Vcl;Str.-D maj.-*Sehr Moderato.*-80m.-Psalm 106:1;I.
Chronica 17:29.
Inserted section: *"Liturg."*
For another version, see Herbst 107.

65.2   [Du solt anbeten vor dem Herrn]

SSAB;2Fl;Str;Clavicembalo.-A maj.-*Affettuoso. con Sordini.*-73m.-
V.Mose 26:10,11; 7:6; 2:7.

65.3   [Wie fein sind deine Hütten]

SSAB;Str. G maj.-18m,incomplete: *"Vide Music zum 7. Sept. 1763
di Gregor."*
Beginning 32m. taken from Gregor's *Wie fein sind deine Hütten*
[Herbst 30.4].

65.4   [Der Herr dein Gott]

SSTTB;2Fl;Str; Clavicembalo.-G maj.-*Sehr Andante.*-72m.-V.Mose 30.9;
III.Mose 26:6; V.Mose 28:6; 7:13.

65.5   [Schreibet euch dis Lied]

B;Str.-D maj.-*Langsam.*-24m.-V.Mose 31:19,21.

65.6   [Nun unser Gott, wir danken dir]

SSAB;2Hns;[2Cl] ;Str.-D maj.-*Gravitaetisch.*-31m.-I.Chronica 17:36.
Clarinet pts.on separate sheet.

66   GREGOR, CHRISTIAN (1723-1801) *Zur Christnacht 1765*

66.1   [Singet dem Herrn alle Lande]

SSAB;[2Hns] ;Str.-D maj.-*Lebhaft.*-86m.-I. Chronica 17:23; Psalms 89:3;
98:3; 19:3; I.Chronica 17:31; Sprüche Salomonis 8:31; V.Mose 33:3.
Hn pts.on separate sheet.
For a variant version, see Herbst 38.1.

66.2   [Tröstet mein Volk—Bereitet dem Herrn]

S/SSAB;Str.-D maj.-*Larghetto. con Sordini; Munter.*-40m.-Jesaia 40:1,2;
Matthäi 21:5; 3:3.
At end: "*Folgt Chorus 2. Zion hörts/Vide Mus. zum 4. May 1761*"
[Herbst 14.2].

66.3   [Hosianna, gelobet sey der]

SSAB/SSAB.-C maj.-27m.-Marci 11:9,10.

66.4   [Wer ist der—Warum ist denn]

S/SSAB;cont.-A min;G maj.-*Recit;Recitativisch.*-74m.-Jesaia 63:1,2,4;
53:5; 63:3; Sacharja 13:6; I.Mose 49:1; Psalms 18:42; 96:13.

66.5   [Machet die Thore weit]

SSAB/SSAB;cont.-G maj.-*Recitativ.*-12m.-Psalm 24:7,8.

66.6   [Machet die Thore weit]

SSAB;cont.-G maj. incomplete: gives chorale incipits for *"Kinder"* and
"Gemeine."-Psalm 24:7,8.

66.7   [Kündlich gross]

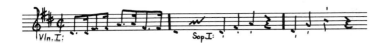

SB;Str.-D maj.-*Largo.*-36m.-I. Timotheum 3:16.

67   GEISLER, JOHANN CHRISTIAN (1729-1815) *Zum 24. Dec. 1765*

67.1   [Ach dass doch die Hülfe—Ach dass du den Himmel]

SS;Str.-D maj.-56m.-Psalm 14:7; Jesaia 64:1.
For an SSAB setting of *Ach dass du den Himmel,* see Herbst 13.5.

67.2   [Hosianna, gelobet sey der]

SS;Str.-D maj.-*Lebhaft.*-35m.-Marci 11:9,10.

67.3   [Christus kommt heraus]

SS;Str.-G maj.- *Andante.*-49m.-Römer 9:5.

67.4   [O süsser Mund! O Glaubens-Grund!]

SS;Str.-A min.-*Andante. mit Sordinen.*-20m.-Hymn.
See Herbst 104.5

68   GEISLER, JOHANN CHRISTIAN (1729-1815) *Text vom 11. u. 12. Jan. 1766*
[Es ist ein Gott]

SSSB;Str.-B-Flat maj.-*Molto Andante.*-59m.-I.Timotheum 2:5,6;
Hymn 134,1 (Rist); Tune 168.

69   GEISLER, JOHANN CHRISTIAN (1729-1815) *Psalm zum Gemein-Fest in Gnadenfrey den 15. Jan.1766*

69.1   [Danket dem Herrn und rühmet]

SSAB;Str.-B-Flat maj.-99m.-Psalms 105:1-3; 95:1; 135:3.
Ends with Tune 185A.

69.2   [Der Herr ist König, und herrlich geschmückt]

SSAB;2Hns;Str.-E-Flat maj.-*Grave.*-31m.-Psalm 93:1.

69.3   [Der Herr wird dich]

SSAB;Str.-E-Flat maj.-34m.-V.Mose 28:9,10.
Losung for January 15, 1766.

69.4   [So spricht der Herr]

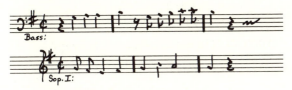

B;Str/SSTT;2Fl;Vcl; Organ(fig. bass).-G maj.-*Sehr Andante.* 41m.-
Jesaia 65:18; Hymn 1141:7,8; Tune 23.

69.5   [Wohl dem Menschen die dir]

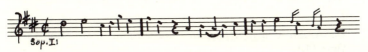

SSAB;"*stromenti concordans.*"-D maj;A maj.-38m.-Psalms 84:6,7; 65:5;
1:1-3; 25:13.

70   GEISLER, JOHANN CHRISTIAN (1729-1815) *Zum 2. Febr. 1766*
      [Der Herr mit euch!]

SSSB;Vln.I,II,III,Basso/SSB;Vla.I,II,Organo.-E-Flat maj.-*Langsam.*-49m.-
Ruth 2:4.
Losung for February 2, 1766.

71   [UNIDENTIFIED] *Zum 25. Mart. 1766*
      [Opfer und Gaben]

SS/SSAB;fig.bass.-G maj.-*Etwas Lebhaft*.-51m.-Ebräer 10:5; Colosser 1:20

72   GREGOR, CHRISTIAN (1723-1801) *Zum Begräbniss des Br. Leonhards am 4. Apr. 1766*
      [Leonhard unser Freund—Ey wie so selig]

SS/SSAB;Fl; Str.-E-Flat maj.-*Affettuoso. con Sordini*.-45m.-
Hymns 937:1,3; 175:4,5; 821:1; Tune 14A.
See also Herbst 73.1: *Gott sey dir gnädig. . . .*

73   GREGOR, CHRISTIAN (1723-1801) *Zum 4. May 1766*

73.1   [Gott sey dir gnädig—Du auserwählte Magd]

S/SSAB;Str.-G maj.-*Affettuoso. con Sordini*.-73m.-I.Mose 43:29; Hymn;
Tune 14A.
Losung and Hymn for May 4, 1766.
See also Herbst 72: *Leonhard unser Freund. . . .*
At end: setting of Tune 14A for keyboard, *"Vorstehende Variation blos auf Clavier."*

73.2   [O angenehme Augenblicke]

SS;2Hns;Str.-F maj.-*Angenehm, u. etwas lebhaft*.-58m.-Hymn 1749,1,
var. (Gregor).

74   GREGOR, CHRISTIAN (1723-1801) *Zum 12. May 1766*
        [Das Haus Gottes ist die Gemeine]

SSAB;Str.-C maj.-*Lebhaft.*-51m.-I.Timotheum 3:15.

75   [UNIDENTIFIED] *Zum 24. Juny 1766*

75.1   [Gemeine sieh dein Leben]

SS;Str.-A-Flat maj.-*Affetto. Andante. con Sordini.*-21m.-Hymn 2054,1
(Kl.Br.Ges.).

75.2   [Wie Er ist, so sind auch wir]

SS;Str.-A-Flat maj.-*Andante. con Sordini.*-11m.-I. Johannis 4:17.
Text for June 24, 1766.

76[.1]   GEISLER, JOHANN CHRISTIAN (1729-1815) *Text am 24. Juny 1766*
        [Wie Er ist, so sind auch wir]

SS;Str.-E-Flat maj.-69m.-I.Johannis 4:17; Hymn 1636,4 (Christian David).
Text and Hymn for June 24, 1766

76[.2]   GEISLER, JOHANN CHRISTIAN (1729-1815) *Zum 17. Aug.* [1766?]
        [Er kennet dich]

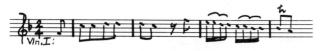

SS;Str.-F maj.-37m.-II.Mose 33:12.

77   GEISLER, JOHANN CHRISTIAN (1729-1815) *Zum P. Seidliz
Begräbniss d. 6. July 1766*

77.1   [(Wir) ruhen hier in einem solchen Frieden]

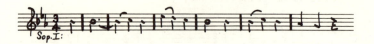

SSAB;Str.-E-Flat maj.-66m.-Hymn 473,2 (Zinzendorf).

77[.2]   [Nun und dann gefällt es Ihm]
Arietta

S;Str.-B-Flat maj.-96m.-Hymn 1715,2 (Zinzendorf).
Alternate text: *Eh mans denkt geschieht es oft.*

77[.3]   [Er schwieg stille]

SSAB;Str.-B-Flat maj.-42m.-Hymn.
Marked *"No. 4"* on ms.

78   HERBST, JOHANNES (1735-1812) *Zum 8. Aug. 1766*
[Nicht hat der Herr euch angenommen]
missing

79   GEISLER, JOHANN CHRISTIAN (1729-1815) *Zum 29. Aug. 1766*
[Wie lieblich sind deine Wohnungen]

SSAB;Str.-G maj.-*Andante.*-99m.-Psalm 84.2-5.

80   GEISLER, JOHANN CHRISTIAN (1729-1815) *Zum 13. Novembr. 1766*

80.1   [Nehmet wahr des Apostels]

SSAB;Str.-A maj.-*Sehr Moderato.*-56m.-Ebräer 3:1.
Text for November 13, 1766.

80.2   [Wir haben einen Hohenpriester]

SSAB;Str.-D maj.-65m.-Ebräer 8:1,2; 9:2.

80.3   [Der Herr ist nahe]

SSAB;Str.-A maj.-*Moderato.*-36m.-Psalm 119:151; Sprüche 8:31.

80.4   [Bringe sie hinein]
        Die Losung zum 13. Nov. 66

SSAB;Str.-A maj.-*Andantino con affetto.*-79m.-II.Mose 15:17.
Losung for November 13, 1766.

80.5   [Freuet euch und seyd fröhlich—Er hat uns geliebet—Lasset uns Ihn
        lieben]

SSAB;[Fl] ;Str;Vcl.-A maj;D maj;D maj.-*Amabile.*-94m.-Zephanja 3:14;
Psalm 136:1; I.Johannis 3:16; 4:19; Offenbarung 5:9.
"Einger Flöten konnen unisono mit den 2 Singstimmen gehen."
Expanded paraphrase of a section from Herbst 25.1 by Christian Gregor.

80.6   [Der Herr ist mein Theil]

SSAB;Str.-D maj.-*Langsam.*-80m.-Klaglieder 3:24; Hohelied 3:4;
Maleachi 4:20; Psalms 73:25; 119:32; I.Corinther 3:22;
Apostelgeschichte 20:28.
Adapted from Gregor's *Der Herr ist mein Theil* [Herbst 14.11].

81   HERBST, JOHANNES (1735-1812) *Zum 13. Nov. 1766*

81.1   [Wir haben ein Fest des Herrn] *"Vide Music zum 25. Mart. 63. No. 1."*
        [Herbst 23.1: Gregor's *Wir haben ein Fest*]

81.2   [Nehmet wahr des Apostels]

SSAB;Str.-F maj.-*Affettuoso zieml. langsam.*-68m.-Ebräer 3:1.
Text for November 13, 1766.

81.3   [Siehe, Er kommt] *"Vide Music 13. Nov. 64, No. 3[No.2?]"*
        [Herbst 46.2: Gregor's *Siehe, Er kommt*]

81.4   [Hosianna, gelobet sey der] *"Vide Music zum 24. Dec. 64, No. 5"*
        [See Herbst 66.3: Gregor's *Hosianna, gelobet sey der*]

81.5   [Wohl dem Volke dess der Herr] *"Vide Music 4. May 63. No. 3"*
        [See Herbst 25.3: Gregor's *Wohl dem Volke, dess der Herr*]

81.6   [Siehe da ein Hütte Gottes] *"Vide Music 4. May 61, No. 11[No.8?]"*
        [Herbst 14.8: Gregor's *Siehe da ein Hütte Gottes*]

81.7   [Bringe uns hinein]

SSAB;Str.-B-Flat maj.-*Moderato.*-40m.-II.Mose 15:17.
Losung for November 13, 1766.

81.8   [Herr unser Gott, du bist nocheben] *"Vide Music zum 17. Aug. 62,
        No. 5"* [See Herbst 19.5: Gregor's *Herr unser Gott, du bist nocheben*]

82   SCHLICHT, LUDOLPH ERNST (1712-1769) *Zum 2. Febr. 1767*

82.1   [Wohl den Menschen die dich]

SSAB;Str; Org(fig.bass).-F maj.-*Ernsthaft.*-44m.-Psalm 84:6.
Losung for February 2, 1767.

82.2   [Lebt indessen wohl]

SSAB;Str; Org(fig.bass).-G maj.-11m.-Hymn.
Marked *"No. 7"* on ms.
See also Herbst 132.3.

83   GEISLER, JOHANN CHRISTIAN (1729-1815) *Zum 2. Febr. 1767*
      [Wohl den Menschen die dich]

SSAB;Str.-B-Flat maj.-76m.-Psalm 84:6.
Losung for February 2, 1767.
Alternate text in red ink: *Wohl denen die Ihn. . . .*

84   HERBST, JOHANNES (1735-1812) *Zum 2. Febr. 1767*
      [Bald wird kommen zu seinem Tempel der Herr]
      missing

85   GEISLER, JOHANN CHRISTIAN (1729-1815) *Losung u. Text am
      14. Mart. 1767 in Herrnhut*
      [Herr wende dich zu uns]

SSAB;Str.-D maj.-*Affettuoso.*-117m.-Psalms 119:132; 89:17; Hymn.
See also Herbst 120.1 and 120.1b.

86   [UNIDENTIFIED] *Zum Gr*[ossen]*Sabb*[ath] *1767*
[Er ist aus dem Lande]

B/SSAB;Str.-F maj.-*Largo.*-20m.-Jesaia 53:8; Matthäi 27:51,52.
Losung for Good Friday, April 17, 1767.

87   GEISLER, JOHANN CHRISTIAN (1729-1815) *Zum 4. May 1767*
[Nach deinem Siege]

SSAB;Str;Fundamento(fig.bass).-F maj.-*Munter.*-78m.-Psalm 110:3;
Hymn.
Text for May 4, 1767.

88   GEISLER, JOHANN CHRISTIAN (1729-1815) *Die Losung vom
4. Juny 1767*
[Herr, lasse mir deine Gnade]

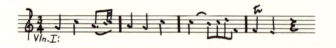

SS;Str;Cembalo/SS;Str;Harpa.-C maj.-*Mässig u. angenehm.*-139m.-
Psalm 119:41; Hymn 1527 (Zinzendorf).
For an arr. for one choir, see Herbst 93.3.

89   HERBST, JOHANNES (1735-1812) *Zum 24. Juny 1767*
[Der Herr liebet die Thore]

SSAB;Str.-F maj.-58m.-Psalm 87:2.
Losung for June 24, 1767.

90   GEISLER, JOHANN CHRISTIAN (1729-1815) *Zum 17. Aug. 1767*

90.1 [Grossen Frieden deinen Kindern]

SSAB; Str; Harpa; Clavecin.-F maj.-64m.

90.2 [Wie herrlich ists]

SSAB;Str;Harpa;Clavecin.-F maj.-*Andante.*-104m.-Hymn 486,1.
Alternate text: *So ruhe wohl.*

90.3 [Aus dem Munde der jungen Kinder]

SSAB;[Str]/SSAB;[Harpa;Clavecin].-F maj.-24m.-Psalm 8:3.
*"Nota die Instrumente gehen mit dem ersten Choro u. die Harpa u.
Clav. mit dem 2. Choro gleich lautend".*

91   GEISLER, JOHANN CHRISTIAN (1729-1815) and JOHANNES
     HERBST (1735-1812) *Zum 29. Aug. 1767*

91.1 [Lobet den Herrn, denn unsern Gott—Ach sängen alle unsre Glieder]
     by Geisler

SSAB;Str.-C maj.-*Etwas munter;Muntrer.*-86m;35m.-Psalm 147:1; Hymn.
Losung and Hymn for August 29, 1767.
See also Herbst 32.2, 32.4, 37.2, and 64.1.

91.2   [Heilig, selig ist die Freundschaft—Denn Er erquicket unsre Seele]
by Herbst

SSAB;Str.-E-Flat maj.-*Affettuoso; Etwas munterer.*-44m;50m.-
Hymn 258,2(Zinzendorf); Psalm 23:3.
Text for August 29, 1767.

92   GEISLER, JOHANN CHRISTIAN (1729-1815) *Zum 29. Aug. 1767
in Barby*
[Lobet den Herrn, denn unsern Gott—Er erquicket unsre Seele]

SSAB;Str.-D maj.-59m.-Psalms 147:1; 23:3.
Losung for August 29, 1767.
See Herbst 42.1 and 118.1.

93   GEISLER, JOHANN CHRISTIAN (1729-1815) *Zum 7. Septembr. 1767*

93.1   [Der im Anfang den Menschen]

SSAB;Str.-F maj.-47m.-Matthäi 19:4; Johannis 3:29; Tunes 228A,159A.

93.2   [Höre Tochter, schaue drauf—Er ist dein Herr]

AB/SSAB;Str.-B-Flat maj;E-Flat maj.-47m.-Psalm 45:11,12.
Losung for September 7, 1767.

93.3   [Herr, lasse mir deine Gnade]

SSAB;Str;keyboard.-B-Flat maj.-95m.-Psalm 119:41;
Hymn 1527(Zinzendorf).
For a transposed version for 2 choirs, see Herbst 88.

93.4   [Opfere Gott Dank]

SSAB;Str.-G maj.-*Molto Andante.*-32m.-Psalm 50:14,23.

93.5   [Wohl dem Volke]

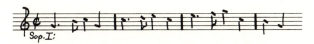

SSAB;Str.-C maj.-42m.-Psalm 144:15; Epheser 5:32.

94   HERBST, JOHANNES (1735-1812) *Zum 29. Sept. 1767*

94.1   [Der Kinder Engel im Himmel sehen]

SATB;Str.-C maj.-*Andante.*-28m.-Matthäi 18:10.

94.2   [Der Engel des Herrn lagert sich]

SATB;Str.-F maj.-*Moderato.*-105m.-Psalms 34:8; 91:11,12; Ebräer 1:14.

95   GEISLER, JOHANN CHRISTIAN (1729-1815) *Die Losung zum 16.
         Octobr. 1767*
         [Lass mich nicht zu Schanden]

SSTB;Str.-D maj.-*Etwas anhaltend langsam.*-117m.-Psalm 119:116; Ebräer 10:19,20.

96   HERBST, JOHANNES (1735-1812) and JOHANN CHRISTIAN GEISLER (1729-1815) *Zum 13. Nov. 1767*

96.1   [Siehe! Finsterniss bedeckte das Erdreich—Aber über dir] by Herbst

SSATB;Str;fig.bass.-D maj.-F maj.-*Grave;Andante.*-14m;40m.-Jesaia 60:2. Losung for November 12, 1767.
Adapted from Pergolesi's *Mass:* "Kyrie." See B XXVIII

96.2   [Erscheine grosser Freund] by Herbst

SSAB;Harpa;keyboard.-C maj;A min.-*Affettuoso.*-33m.-
Hymn 1196,1(Zinzendorf).
Hymn for November 12, 1767.

96.3   [Komm weide du dein Volk] *"Vide Music zum 13. Nov. 1764"*
[Herbst 46.1: Gregor's *Komm weide du dein Volk*]
"Choral: Dein Volk ergibt sich deinen treuen Händen" [Hymn 966,3]

96.4   [Der Herr ist unser König] by Herbst

SSAB/SSAB;Str.-D maj.-*Moderato.*-61m.-Jesaia 33:22; Psalms 72:12,13; 149:4; 115:12; 125:2; 117:2.
See Herbst 449
At end: *"Choral. Pater familias hat sich ins Herz geprägt."*

96.5   [Dein Recht und dein Licht] by Herbst

B/SSAB;Str.-D min.-*Larghetto.*-64m.-V.Mose 33:8.
Losung for November 13, 1767.
Adapted from Handel's *The Messiah:* "But who may abide."
At end: *"Choral. Er wohnt in unsern Hütten."*

96.6   [Gott stehet in der Gemeine—Fürchte dich nicht] by Geisler

SSAB;Str.-D maj.-*Langsam, oder Andante.*-78m.-Psalm 82:1;
Jesaia 40:11; Zephanja 3:13; Lucä 12:32.
At end: *"Gem. Du Herzens Lamm, du treuer Mann."* [Hymn 1099,8]

96.7   [Bringet dem Namen] by Geisler

T/SA;Str;keyboard.-D maj.-*Andante.*-31m.-Psalm 149:5; Hymn; Tune 22B.
Psalm [T] alternates with chorale [SA]

96[b]   GEISLER, JOHANN CHRISTIAN (1729-1815) *Zum 13. Nov. 1767*

96[b].1 [Siehe! Finsterniss bedecket das Erdreich—Aber über dir]

B/SSAB;Str.-D min;D maj.-43m.-Jesaia 60:2.
Losung for November 12, 1767.

96[b].2 [Erscheine grosser Freund]

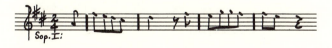

SSAB;Str.-D maj.-*Molto Andante.*-31m.-Hymn 1196,1(Zinzendorf).
Hymn for November 12, 1767.

96[b].3 [Komm weide du dein Volk] *"Vide Br. Gregors Compos. de anno. 1764"* [Herbst 46.1]
"Gem. Dein Volck ergibt sich." [Hymn 966,3]

96[b].4 [Der Herr ist unser König]

SSAB;Str.-D maj.-69m.-Jesaia 33:22; Psalms 72:12,13; 149:4; 115:12; 125:2; 117:2.
At end: *"Gem. Pater familias."*

96[b].5 [Dein Recht und dein Licht]

T/SSAB;Str.-A maj.-83m.-V.Mose 33:8.
Losung for November 13, 1767.
At end: *"Gem. Er wohnt in unsern Hütten."*

96[b].6 [Gott stehet in der Gemeine] *"Vide Music 13. Nov. in G[naden]fr[ey]"* [Herbst 96.6?]
"Gem. Du Herzens Lamm! du treuer Mann." [Hymn 1099,8]

96[b].7 [Bringet dem Namen]

TT/SSAB;Str.-B-Flat maj.-*Frölich.*-73m.-Psalm 149:5; Hymn; Tune 22L.
Psalm [TT] alternates with chorale [SSAB]

96[b].8 [Wer sich rühmen will] *"Vide Music vom 13. Nov. 1764 di Gregor"* [Herbst 46.3]
"Gemeine: Der Eltesten ganze Schaar" [Hymn 710,5]

96[b].9 [Lobsingt, lobsinget Gott]

SSAB;Str/SSAB;Str.-E-Flat maj.-46m.-Psalms 47:7; 100:5; 91:4; 147:13; Jesaia 24:23.

97   HERBST, JOHANNES (1735-1812) *Zum 24. Decembr. 1767*

97.1   *"Vide Music zum 24. Dec. 1765. No. 3"* [Herbst 67.3?]

97.2   [Singet dem Herrn ein neues Lied. Ein tag]

SSAB;Str.-D maj.-*Munter.*-65m.-Psalm 19:3; Johannis 8:42;
II.Samuelis 22:10.
At end: *"Choral: Unser Gott ohne Vergleich an Huld."*

97.3   [Kommt herzu, lasset uns]

SSAB;Str.-G maj.-*Andante.*-108m.-Psalms 94:1,2,6; 98:3;
Joel 2:20; Lucä 1:47,68,69,77,78.
At end: *"Choral: Die wahre Gnaden-Sonne:"* [Hymn 87]

97.4   *"Vide Music zum 24. Dec. 1765, No. 5. Hosianna"* [Herbst 66.3?]
"Choral. Gott der Vater der Ewigkeit" [Hymn 1738]

97.5   *"Vide Music zum 24. Dec. 1765, No. 9. Kündlich gross"* [Herbst 66.7?]
"Choral. O verehrungswürdger Tag." [Hymn 42?]

97.6   [Uns ist ein Kind geboren]

SSAB;Str.-A maj.-*Frölich, doch nicht zu geschwind.*-102m.-Jesaia 9:6,7.
Losung for December 24, 1767.
At end: *"Gem. Das ewige Licht das war sein Kleid."*[Hymn 1738,2]
"Kinder: Ave Christ-Kindlein."[Herbst 5.2].

[97.6b] [Uns ist ein Kind geboren]
SSAB/SSAB;[Str].-A maj.-*Lebhaft, doch nicht zu geschwind.*
Vocal score.
An arr. for 2 choirs of Herbst 97.6.

97.7   [Meine Seele erhebe den Herrn]
Chorus.

SSAB/SSAB;[Str].-F maj.-96m.-Lucä 1:46; 2:30-32; Ebräer 10:5;
Colosser 1:20.
"Die Instrumente gehen mit den Singstimmen."
At end: *"Gem. Herr durch deinen heiligen Leichnam."* [Hymn 1184,2]

97.8   [Siehe, das ist Gottes Lamm]

S;Str.-D min.-*Langsam, mit Sordinen.*-35m.-Johannis 1:29.
At end: *"Kinder: Ave ihr Triebe"* [Herbst 5.1, with
alternate text; see also Salem Congregation Collection, S5.2.]

[97.8b]   [Siehe, das ist Gottes Lamm]

SS;Str.-D min.-*Langsam, mit Sordinen.*
Vocal score.
An arr. for 2 sopranos of Herbst 97.8.

97.9   [O du zu meinem Trost]

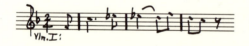

SS;Str.-F maj.-*Affettuoso.*-112m.-Hymn.
At end: *"Gem. Und schick uns dein Flämmlein her."*

97.10   [Freuet euch und seyd frölich]

SSAB;Str.-B-Flat maj.-*Frölich, nicht zu geschwind.*-118m.-
Psalms 45:3; 104:2; 72:19.
At end: *"Kinder: Das ewige Licht ging da herein"* [Hymn 56,4]

97.11   [Und alsbald war—Ehre sey Gott in der Höhe]
Recitativ-Chorus

B recit;Str;SSAB;Str/SSAB;Str.-D min;D maj.-Mässig.-49m.-Lucä 2:13,14.
An arr. of Gregor's *Ehre sey Gott in der Höhe.*
See also Herbst 13.10 and Herbst 22.3

98   HERBST, JOHANNES (1735-1812) *Zum 6. Jan. 1768*

98.1   [Das Volk das im Finstern wandelt]
missing

98.2   [Lobet den Herrn alle Heiden]

SATB;2Fl[or Ob];2Hns;Str;Fondamento.-C maj.-*Munter, nur nicht
zu geschwind.*-56m.-Psalms 117:1; 22:28.
For another version, see Herbst [98b.2]

[98b]   HERBST, JOHANNES (1735-1812) *Zum 6. Jan.* [17]68

[98b.1]   [Singet dem Herrn in vollen Chören]
"Parodie auf Rolle's Lobgesang der ersten Eltern aus dem Tod Abels"

S;keyboard. E Flat maj.-31m.
See Herbst 214b[.2]
Not entered in Herbst's book of texts.

[98b.2]   [Lobet den Herrn alle Heiden]

SSAB;Str.-C maj.-*Munter, doch nicht zu geschwind.*-54m.-Psalms 117:1;
22:28.
For another version, see Herbst 98.2.
Not entered in Herbst's book of texts.

99   HERBST, JOHANNES (1735-1812) *Zum Knabenfest am 10. Jan. 1768*

99.1   [Jesus ging mit seinen Eltern]

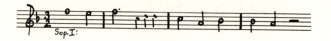

SSAB.-F maj.-*Langsam.*-incomplete: *"Vide Continuat, Music zum Knabenfest 1765"* [Herbst 50a].-Lucä 2:51,52.

99.2   [Herr wende dich zu ihnen]

SSAB;Str.-D maj.-*Andante.*-177m.-Psalms 119:132,133,41,54; 103:14; 127:4.

100   GEISLER, JOHANN CHRISTIAN (1729-1815) *Zum Gemein-Fest in Gnadenfrey am 13. Januar 1768*
        [Lobet den Herrn, denn Er ist]
        Chorus

SSAB.-G min.-20m.-Psalm 135:3.

100.1   [Das ist der Tag]

SSAB;Str.-B-Flat maj.-43m.-Psalms 118:24; 149:2.
For another version, see Gregor's *Gelobet sey der Herr—Das ist ein Tag* [Herbst 22.4]

100.2   [Der Herr hat wohlgefallen]

SSATB;Str.-B-Flat maj.-78m.-Psalm 149:4.

100.3   [Der Gerechte wird blühen]

SSAB;Str.-F maj.-75m.-Psalm 92:13-16.

100.4   [Höre zu Josua]

SSAB;Str.-C maj.;G maj.-52m.

100.5   [Wer kann die grossen Thaten]

B/SSAB;Str.-D maj.-37m.-Psalm 106:2.

101   GEISLER, JOHANN CHRISTIAN (1729-1815) *Zum 26. Jan. 1768*
[Das herrliche Evangelium]

SS;Str.-E Flat maj.-59m.

102   HERBST, JOHANNES (1735-1812) *Zum 2. Febr. 1768*

102.1   *"Chorus 1. Mel. Mein Salomo"* [Tune 114]
"Gem. Du segnest ja so gern" [Hymn 1772, Kl. Brr. Gesb.]

102.2   [Wir wollen der Güte des Herrn gedenken]

SSAB;Str.-C maj.-*Larghetto.*-108m.-Psalms 109:31; 147:3;
Jesaia 40:29; 61.
At end: *"Choral: O Herr, welch ein weites Feld."*

102.3   [Wie sicher wohnet]

SSAB;Str.-A min.-*Angenehm u. langsam.*-67m.-V.Mose 33:12;
Josua 1:13; Psalm 128:5,6.
At end: *"Gem. Auf Erd in Christlicher Gemein"*

102.4   [Auf die Einsamen]

SSAB;Str.-F maj.-*Affettuoso.*-40m.-Psalm 130:5,6.
Alternate text in red ink.
At end: *"Gem. Du unsrer Herzens Wünsche Ziel"*

102.5   [Wir sind vertrauet]

SS;Str.-E-Flat maj.-*Langsam u. mit Affect.*-53m.
At end: *"Gem. Heilig selig ist die Freundschaft."*

102.6   *"Vide Music zum 2. Febr. 1765, no. 9: Ich weiss an wen ich gläube"*
         [Herbst 54.3]
         "Gem. Das Herze des geweisse"

102.7   *"Chorus ohne Instrumente: Wohl denen, die in deinem Hause wohnen/
         Vid Music zum 22. Nov. 1763, No. 5"* [Herbst 31.5]
         "Gem. Wo seit so viel Tausend Jahren" [Hymn 1719]

102.8   *"Chorus ohne Instrumente: Der Herr des Friedens gebe euch
         Friede/Vid. Mus. ulto. Dec. 1763. No. 2."* [Herbst 33.2]
         "Gem. Das walt der es heisst"

103   GEISLER, JOHANN CHRISTIAN (1729-1815) *Zum 2. Febr. 1768*
       [Der Herr hat uns gerufen]

SSAB;Str.-G maj.-87m.-Ezechiel 34:11,12,14,16.

104   HERBST, JOHANNES (1735-1812) *Zum grossen Sabbath 1768*

104.1   [Du der mit Blut und Wunden]
         Choral.

Tune 151A, with fig.bass.-38m.
From Karl Heinrich Graun's *Der Tod Jesu*, no.1.
At end: *"Gem. Wir sind deine Tod verflichtet."*

104.2   [Siehe, das ist Gottes Lamm]
         Choro.

T;Vln;fig.bass.-B-Flat maj.-25m.-Johannis 1:29; Hymn 106,1-3; Tune 261.
A reduction of Karl Heinrich Graun's *Siehe, das ist Gottes Lamm.*
At end: *"Gem: Ich stehe da u. weine/Dis dur."*

104.3   [Er hat in den Tagen]

SSAB;Str.-C min.-*Largo.*-28m.-Ebräer 5:7.
Alternate text incipit: *Christus hat am Tage.*
At end: *"Gem: Da Er uns unsre Wahl/G dur."*

104.4   [Schaut auf und seht]

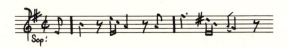

S;fig.bass.-E min.-*Largo e piano.*-14m.
Adapted from the Tenor aria "Behold and see" in Handel's
The Messiah.

104.5   [Ein Würmlein roth]

S;keyboard.-G min.-*Andante.*-62m.-Hymn.
Adapted from Karl Heinrich Graun's *Der Tod Jesu*, no. 23:
"Ihr Augen weint."
See Herbst 67.4
At end: *"Gem. Ein Herz des an dich glaubt."*

104.6   [Er war verachtet]

S;keyboard.-E-Flat maj.-*Largo.*-67m.
Adapted from the Alto aria "He was despised" in Handel's *The Messiah*.
See Herbst 290.1

104.7   *Choral.*

Mel.and fig.bass.-C min.-11m.-textless.
At end: *"Gem. Die Geisseln u. die Banden/B dur."*

104.8   [Er ist erschienen]

SSAB;Str.-F maj.-*Andante.*-74m.-Ebräer 9:26; 5:3; Colosser 1:20.

104[.9] [*Choral.*]

SSAB;fig.bass.-C min.-11m.-textless.

105   HERBST, JOHANNES (1735-1812) *Zum Ostertage 1768*

105[.1] [Spricht Jesus zu ihr: Weib was weinest du?]

S;Str.-E-Flat maj.-*Langsam. con Sordini.*-13m.-Johannis 20:15.

105[.2] [Spricht Jesus zu ihr: Maria! Da wandte sie sich]

S;Str.-E-Flat maj.-21m.-Johannis 20:16.

106   GEISLER, JOHANN CHRISTIAN (1729-1815) *Zum 25. Apr. 1768*

106.1   [Beglüktes Herz!]

SSAB;Str;Clavier.-D maj.-*Tempo moderato.*-78m.-Hymn 633.

106.2   [Drum segnet Er]
       Duetto

SS;Str/AB;Vcl;Clavier.-B min.-*Animoso.*-51m.-Hymn.

106.3   [Sein Gnadenblick macht dir]

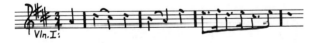

SSAB;Str;Clavier.-D maj.-*Un poco Vivace.*-73m.-Hymn 665,3(Gregor).

107   GEISLER, JOHANN CHRISTIAN (1729-1815) *Zum 25. Apr. 1768*
      [Ich will vor dem Herrn spielen]

S/SSAB;Str;Harpa;Clavier.-D maj.-*Moderato.*-77m.
For another version, see Herbst 65.1.

108   GEHRA, AUGUST HEINRICH (1715-1785) *Zum 25. Apr. 1768*

108.1   [Den schönsten Gruss]

SSAA;Str;2 Harps.-D maj.-*Un poco Andante.*-84m.-Hymn; Tune 14A.

108.2   [Gott sey dir gnädig und segne]

SSAA;Str;2 Harps.-B min.-*Adagio.*-27m.-Psalm 67:2.

109   HERBST, JOHANNES (1735-1812) and JOHANN CHRISTIAN GEISLER (1729-1815) *Zum 4. May 1768*

109.1   [Friede sey mit euch!] by Herbst

S;Str.-C maj;A min;E maj.-*Etwas langsam, mit Affect.*-23m.-
III.Johannis 15.
Alternate text: *Kyrie eleison.*
Tune 14A incipit after each section.

109.2   [Er kennet dich] by Herbst

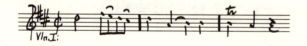

SSAB;Str.-D maj.-*Affettuoso.*-62m.-II.Mose 33:12.

109.3   [Er ist der Heilige] by Geisler

SSAB;Str.-D min;F maj.-*Gravitaetisch.*-47m.

109.4   [Mein Herz freuet sich] by Geisler

SSAB;Str.-F maj.-*Frölich, doch nicht zu hurtig.*-103m.-Psalm 13:6; Hymn.
Losung and Hymn for May 4, 1768.

109.5   *"Vid. Partitur No. 95"* [Herbst 95]

109.6   *"Vid. Partitur No. 87"* [Herbst 87]

110   HERBST, JOHANNES (1735-1812) *Zum 24. Juny 1768*
       [Gib mir dein Herz]

SSAB;Str.-A min.-*Langsam.*-75m.-Hymn 406,1(Gregor).

111   HERBST, JOHANNES (1735-1812) *Zum 17. Aug. 1768*
       [Er ist der grosse Hirte]

SSAB;Str.-C maj.-*Etwas Munter.*-34m. Ebräer 13:20.

112   GEISLER, JOHANN CHRISTIAN (1729 1815) *Zum 29. Aug. 1768*

112.1   [Freue dich und sey frölich]

SSAB;Str.-F maj.-*Vivace.*-91m.-Sacharja 2:10.
Losung for August 29, 1768.

112.2   [Er kennet die Seinen]
         Text.

SSAB;Str.-F maj.-26m.-II.Timotheum 2:19
Text for August 29, 1768.

113   KERSTEN, ?? *Zum 29. Aug. 1768*

113.1   [Freue dich und sey frölich]
Arietta a 2 Canti o Tenori 2 Viola e Organo

SS(orTT);Str;Organo.-B-Flat maj.-*Poco Andante.*-153m.-
Sacharja 2:10; Hymn 1353,3.
Losung and Hymn for August 29, 1768.

113.2   [Er kennet die Seinen]
Coro.

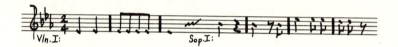

S/SATB;Str;Fondamento.-E-Flat maj.-*Poco Adagio.*-102m.-
II.Timotheum 2:19; Hymn.
Text and Hymn for August 29, 1768.

114   GREGOR, CHRISTIAN (1723-1801) *Losung u. Text am 29.*
August 1768

114.1   [Freue dich und sey fröhlich]

SSAB;Str.-B-Flat **maj.**-*Munter doch nicht zu geschwind.*-46m.-
Sacharja 2:10.
Losung for August 29, 1768.
See also Herbst 14.6.

114.2   [Er kennet die Seinen]

SSAB;Str.-A maj.-*Lebhaft, doch ohne die Punkte zu sehr zu marquiren.*-
35m.-II.Timotheum 2:19.
Text for August 29, 1768.

115   HERBST, JOHANNES (1735-1812) *Zum 7. Sept. 1768*
[Du bist der Herr unser Gott]

SSAB;Str.-B-Flat maj.-*Moderato.*-107m.-Psalms 32:8; 61:8; 28:9; 90:14;
119:54; 135; 37:4; Jesaia 49:2; V.Mose 4:29; Daniel 9:18.

116   [UNIDENTIFIED] *Text am 7. Septembr. 1768*
[Er, den man uns nicht erst nennt]

SSB;Str.-B-Flat maj.-*Affettuoso.*-62m.-I.Petri 1:19.
Text for September 7, 1768.

117   GEISLER, JOHANN CHRISTIAN (1729-1815) *Zur Einweyhung des neuen Saals in Zeit. d. 20. Oct. 1768*

117.1   [Herr! ich habe lieb die Stätte]

SSAB,2Fl;2Hns;Str.-D maj.-*Munter.*-104m.-Psalms 26:8; 84:3; 27:4;
26:7; 43:3,4.
Catalog of the Lititz collection, prepared by Herbst in 1795, cites
Christian Gottfried Geisler as the composer.

117.2   [Daselbst wollt ich dich]

SSAB;2Fl;Str.-G maj.-*Moderato.*-98m.-Psalms 63:5,6; 51:16,17; 54:8.

117.3   [Preise Jerusalem den Herrn]

SSAB;2Fl;2Hns;Str.-D maj.-*Munter.*-103m.-Psalms 147:12;
148:12,13; 149:1,3; 150:2-6.

118   GEISLER, JOHANN CHRISTIAN (1729-1815) *Zum 13. Novembr 1768*
Choral: Gott wolln wir loben

SSAB;2Hns;Str.-F maj.-18m.-Hymn 940; Tune 520.

118.1   [Singet dem Herrn ein neues Lied und lobet]

SSAB/SSAB;2Hns;Str.-F maj.-62m.-Psalms 96:1,2; 100:2,3.
For another version, see Herbst 42.1. See also Herbst 92.

118.2   [Er ist der Hohepriester]

SSAB;4Trpt(SATB);Str;Fondamento.-C maj.-*Grave.*-81m.-
Ebräer 10:21.
Supplied with organ reduction of trpt. pts.

118.3   [Das Haus Gottes ist die Gemeine]

SSAB;Str.-B-Flat maj.-41m.-I.Timotheum 3:15.

118.4   [Sein Name ist eine ausgeschüttete Salbe]

SSAB;Str.-E-Flat maj.-*Amabile.*-84m.-Hohelied 1:3; Colosser 3:17.

118.5   [Siehe wie gerne sie hingehn]

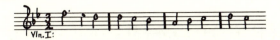

SSAB;Str.-B-Flat maj.-52m.-Psalm 42:5.

119   HERBST, JOHANNES (1735-1812) *Zum 8. Januar. 1769*

119.1   [Da Jesus 12 Jahr alt war]
Recitativ. Arioso.

AB;Str.-D maj.-*Largo.*-24m.-Lucä 2:42,46.
Marked *"No. 2"* on ms.
At end: *"Gem. Wie viel zum Vorbild/3 Verse"* [Hymn 1235].

119.2   [Alle die Ihm zuhöreten]
Recitativ.

S;continuo.-A min.-*Largo.*-4m.-Lucä 2:47.
Marked *"No. 3"* on ms.
At end: *"Gem. Wer lerne von dir, was sich gehört."*

119.3   [Und zu seinen Eltern]
Recitativ. Arioso.

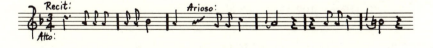

A;Str.-F min;C maj.-*Largo.*-19m.-Lucä 2:49.
Marked *"No. 4"* on ms.
At end: *"Gem. Nimm du mein Herz"*

119.4   [Er ging mit seinen Eltern]
    Recitativ. Arioso.

B;Str.-C maj;D min.-10m.-Lucä 2:51.
Marked *"No. 5"* on ms.
At end: *"Gem. Deine Unterthänigkeit/Jesus nahm zu* [Herbst 50, 51?]
Gem. Ach gib an deinem kostbaren Heil [Hymn 446,5]/*Herr wende
dich zu ihnen* [Herbst 99.2, 120.1?]/*Gem. Dazu sprich selbst das Amen/
Kindlein bleibet bey ihm* [Herbst 55.2, 443?]/*Gem. Die wir uns allhier
beysammen finden* [Hymn 622,4]."

120   HERBST, JOHANNES (1735-1812) *Zum 2. Febr. 1769*

120.1   [Herr wende dich zu ihnen]

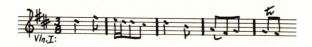

SSAB;Str.-D maj.-*Affettuoso.*-58m.-Psalm 119:132.
Adapted from J. C. Geisler's *Herr wende dich zu uns* [Herbst 85].
See also Herbst 120.1b
At end: *"Gem. Der König wende sich"* [Hymn 1089,3].

120.2   [Von Ihm geht die Kraft]

A;Str.-C maj.-*Poco Largo.*-50m.-Lucä 5:17.
Text for February 2, 1769.
Alternate text: *Der Herr ist in Seinem heiligen Tempel.*
At end: *"Gem. Du bist, o Seelenbräutigam"* [Hymn 1630,2].

120.3   *"Auf die Einsamen/ Vide Music zum 2. Febr. 1768, no. 4"*
    [Herbst 102.4]
    "Gem. Ja komm in aller Eile"

120.4   *"Wie sicher wohnet/ Vide Music zum 2. Febr. 1768, no. 3"*
    [Herbst 102.3]
    "Gem. Herr dein Blut vergiessen" [Hymn 1731,3]/ *O Gott unsers Lebens*

120.5   [Der Herr der deinen Mund—Er hat sich deiner herzlich angenommen]
    Recitativ. Arioso.

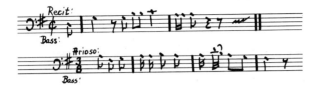

SB;Str.-G maj;E min.-66m.-Psalm 103:5.

[Dankt mit Thränen]
Aria. di Agricola

A;Str.-E maj;C-sharp min;E maj.-*Adagio ma non troppo. con Sordini;*
Allegro. senza Sordini;Adagio. con Sordini.-20m;20m;20m.-Hymn.
At end: *"Gem. O Schöpfer unsrer Seel."*

120.6   [Herr Zebaoth! Gott deiner Heere]

SATB;Str.-E maj.-*Largo.*-35m.
Adapted from Karl Heinrich Graun's *Der Tod Jesu,* no. 24.
At end: *"Gem. Alles sage Amen den Herrn zu loben"* [Hymn 1731,4].

120.7   [Gnade und Friede sey über euch]
Chorus.

SSAB;Str.-A maj.-*Moderato.*-54m.-II.Timotheum 4:8; I.Petri 5:14.

120.1b GEISLER, JOHANN CHRISTIAN (1729-1815) *Zum 31. Aug. 1778*
[Herr wende dich zu ihnen]

SSAB;2Fl;Str.-D maj.-*Affettuoso.*-117m.-Psalms 119:132; 89:17; Hymn.
For another version without flutes, see Herbst 85.
See also Herbst 120.1.

121   HERBST, JOHANNES (1735-1812) *Zum Ostertage 1769*
           [Ich werde auffahren]

         SSAB;Str.-E-Flat maj.-*Etwas langsam. con Sordini.*-17m.-Johannis 20:17.

122   HERBST, JOHANNES (1735-1812) and JOHANN CHRISTIAN
           GEISLER (1729-1815) *Zum 4. May 1769*

122.1   [Lob and Preis und Ehre! dem Hohenpriester] by Herbst

         SSAB.-E-Flat maj.-17m.-Ebräer 8:1; 9:12.

122.2   [Lob und Preis und Ehre! dem unschuldigen] by Herbst

         SSAB;fig.bass.-E-Flat maj.-13m.
         Alternate text: *Lob und Ehre und Anbetung.*

122.3   [An einem Tage] by Geisler

         SSAB;Str.-B-Flat maj.-89m.-III.Mose 16:30.
         Losung for May 4, 1769.

122.4   [Dieser Jesus, welcher von euch—Wenn du, liebster Jesu] by Geisler

SSAB;Str.-B-Flat maj;E-Flat maj.-[no tempo marking] ;*Amabile.*-
129m.-Apostelgeschichte 1:11; Hymn 161,4 (Zinzendorf).
Text and Hymn for May 4, 1769.

122.5   [Lob und Preis und Ehre! dem Menschen-Sohn] by Herbst

SSAB.-B-Flat maj.-14m.
On back of ms: Tune 158, with fig. bass.

123   HERBST, JOHANNES (1735-1812) *Losung zum 22. May 1769*
[Freue dich deiner Hütten—Gott sey Dank]

SSAB;Harpa;Clavicembalo;Str.-D maj.-*Lebhaft.*-81m.-V.Mose 33:18;
Hymn 2283 [Herrnhuter Gesangbuch, III. Zugabe].
Losung and Hymn for May 22, 1769.

124   GEISLER, JOHANN CHRISTIAN (1729-1815)
[Der Herr ist barmherzig]

SSAB;Str.-F maj.-64m-Jacobi 5:11; Hymn 595,1 (Zinzendorf).
Text and Hymn for August 17, 1769.

125   GEISLER, JOHANN CHRISTIAN (1729-1815) *Zum 29. Aug. 1769*

125.1   [Man soll keinen Frevel]

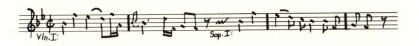

SSAB;Str.-B-Flat maj.-57m.-Jesaia 60:18; Hymn 1190,1 (Zinzendorf).
Losung and Hymn for August 29, 1769.

125.2   [Er ist der Anfänger]

SSAB;Str.-F maj.-71m.-Ebräer 12:2.
Text for August 29, 1769.

126   HERBST, JOHANNES (1735-1812) *Zum 7. Sept. 1769*
       [Alle deine Kinder]

SS/SSAB;Str.-F maj.-*Etwas langsam.*-56m.-Jesaia 54:13.
Losung for September 7, 1769.

127[.1] GREGOR, CHRISTIAN (1723-1801) *Zum 4. May 1770*
       [Seine Taube in den Steinrizen]

SS;Str.-A maj.-*Langsam und doch nicht schläfrig. Con Sordini.*-
84m.-Hohelied 2:14.

127[.2] [Mein Freund ist mein]

SS;Str.-A min.-*Andante.*-86m.-Hohelied 2:16.

127[.3] GEISLER, JOHANN CHRISTIAN (1729-1815) *Zum 4. May 1770*
       [Seine Taube in den Felsritzen]

S;Str;keyboard sketch.-D maj.-*Affettuoso e Lento.*-93m.-Hohelied 2:14.

127[.4] [Mein Freund ist mein]

S;Str.-D maj.-*Amabile.*-37m.-Hohelied 2:16.
Adapted from Gregor's SSAB setting [Herbst 14.14].

128   GEISLER, JOHANN CHRISTIAN (1729-1815) *Zum 29. Aug. 1770*
[Der Gott des Friedens]

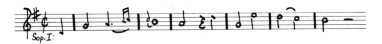

SSAB;fig.bass.-G maj.-41m.-I.Thessalonicher 5:23,24.

129   HERBST, JOHANNES (1735-1812) *Zum 29. Aug. 1770*
[Du hast dich meiner Seele]

SB;Str.-B-Flat maj.-*Etwas langsam.*-95m.-Jesaia 38:17; Hymn 755,6.
Losung and Hymn for August 29, 1770.

130   HERBST, JOHANNES (1735-1812) *Zum 7. Sept. 1770*
[Ich will singen von der Gnade]

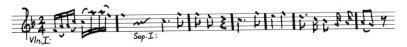

SSAB;Str.-F maj.-*Munter, nicht zu geschwind.*-71m.-Psalm 89:2.
Losung for September 7, 1770.
At end: "*Gem. So kriegt Jesus Jehovah durch die Gemeine u. Chöre
manch dankbares Hallelujah u. gläubigs Miserere*" [Hymn 1044,9].

131   GEISLER, JOHANN CHRISTIAN (1729-1815) *Zum 13. Novembr. 1770*
[Gott hat Christum Jesum]

SSAB;Str.-A maj.-*Andante.*-99m.-Römer 3:25; Hymn 1622,5.
Losung and Hymn for November 13, 1770

132   HERBST, JOHANNES (1735-1812) *Zum 2. Febr. 1771*

132.1   [Abraham blieb stehen—Du mit Blut]

SSAB;Str.-E-Flat maj.-*Affettuoso.*-42m.-I.Mose 18:22; Hymn.
Losung and Hymn for February 2, 1771.

132.2   [Alle Dinge sind mir—Auch wir sind]

B/SSAB;Str.-C maj.-*Langsam.*-70m.-Matthäi 11:27; Hymn; Tune 22B.
Text and Hymn for February 2, 1771.
Alternate text: *Einer ist euer Meister.*
See also Herbst 285.2

132.3   [Lebt indessen wohl]

SSAB; Str.-G maj.-15m.-Hymn.
Expanded version of Schlicht's setting of the same text [Herbst 82.2].

132b   HERBST, JOHANNES (1735-1812) *Zum 25. Apr. 1771*
[Lasst Elisabeth]

SSAB;Str;Harpa.-D maj.-*Munter.*-43m.-Hymn.
Alternate text: *Nun so geht in Seiner Freude.*

133a   GEISLER, JOHANN CHRISTIAN (1729-1815) *Zum 4. May 1771*

133a.1 [Jauchze du Tochter]

SSAB;Str.-F maj.-*Lebhaft.*-132m.-Zephanja 3:14,15.
Losung for May 4, 1771.

133a.2 [Ich will euch wieder sehen]

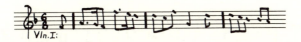

S;Str.-F maj.-*Affettuoso.*-55m.-Johannis 16:22.
Text for May 4, 1771.

133b GEISLER, JOHANN CHRISTIAN (1729-1815) *Zum 4. May 1771*
[Gott man lobet dich]

SSAB;Str.-B-Flat maj.-75m.-Psalm 65:2.

134 HERBST, JOHANNES (1735-1812) *Zum 29. Aug. 1771*
[So ihr bleiben]

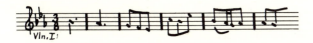

S;Str.-E-Flat maj.-*Mit affect, nicht zu langsam.*-80m.-Johannis 8:31,32.
Text for August 29, 1771.

135 HERBST, JOHANNES (1735-1812) *Zum 7. Sept. 1771*

135[.1] [Hüte dich nur]

SSAB;Str.-B-Flat maj.-*Moderato.*-67m.-V.Mose 4:9.
Losung for September 7, 1771.
Marked No. "2" on ms.

135[.2] [Sie werden alle]

SSAB;Str.-C min.-*Etwas langsam.*-28m.-Johannis 6:45.
Text for September 7, 1771.
Marked No. *"4"* on ms.

135.3 [Du hast durch deine Schöpfers]

SSAB;Str.-F maj.-*Vivace.*-39m.-Hymn 290,5; Tune 22B.
For another version, see Herbst 30.1a.
See also Herbst 55.1.

136 GEISLER, JOHANN CHRISTIAN (1729-1815) *Zum 13. Nov. 1771*

136.1 [Der Herr ist in Seinem heiligen Tempel]

SSAB;2Bn;Str.-C maj.-64m.-Habbacuc 2:20.
Losung for November 13, 1771.
"Fagotti oder mit einem Gamben Register auf der Orgel."

136.2 [Gelobet sey der Herr, der Gott]

SSAB;Str.-D maj.-*Vivace.*-18m.-I.Chronica 17:36.
See also Herbst 22.4.

137 GEISLER, JOHANN CHRISTIAN (1729-1815) *Zum 11. Decembr. 1771*

137.1 [Wie sich die Sündrin]

SS;2Vlns;Harpa;Clavicembalo.-D maj.-81m.-Hymn.
Alternate text: *Gehab dich in der Heimath* [Hymn 1747,9].

137.2   [Schönstes Herz!]

SS;2Vlns;Harpa;Clavicembalo.-D maj.-*Affettuoso*.-74m.-Hymn.

138   GREGOR, CHRISTIAN (1723-1801) *Zum 31. Dec. 1771*
[Du solt anbeten vor dem Herrn]

SSAB.-C maj.-*Etwas langsam*.-45m.-V. Mose 26:10,11; 7:6; 2:7.

139   GEISLER, JOHANN CHRISTIAN (1729-1815) *Zum 13. Jan. 1772*
[Herr unser Gott, siehe]

SSAB;Str;fig.bass.-B-Flat maj.-*Grave*.-51m.-Daniel 9:17; Psalm 106:4,5.

140   GEISLER, JOHANN CHRISTIAN (1729-1815) *Zum 25. Mart. 1772*
[Die Menschheit Jesu]

SSAB;Str;Harpa.-F maj.-94m.-Hymn.

141   VERBEEK, JOHANN RENATUS (1748-1820) *An Ostern 1772*
[Der Herr ist auferstanden]

TB/SATB;Str;fig. bass.-D maj.-*Allegro. Vivace*.-83m.-Lucä 24:34;
II.Timotheum 2:8; Offenbarung 1:18.

142   HERBST, JOHANNES (1735-1812) *Losung zum 4. May 1772*
[Sie werden weder hungern]

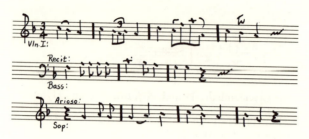

SB;Str.-F maj.-*Affettuoso.*-82m.-Jesaia 49:10.

143   GEISLER, JOHANN CHRISTIAN (1729-1815) *Zum 4. May 1772*
[Sie werden weder hungern]

T/SSAB;Str;Vcl;Harpa;Cembalo;Fondamento.-A maj.-156m.-
Jesaia 49:10; Hymn 1728,5.
Losung and Hymn for May 4, 1772.

144   HERBST, JOHANNES (1735-1812) *Zum 17. Juny 1772*

144.1   [Setze mich wie ein Siegel]

SSAB;Str.-A min.-*Langsam.*-84m.-Hohelied 8:6.
Losung for June 17, 1772.

144.2   [Ihr seyd der Tempel]

SSAB;Str.-C maj.-*Largo.*-84m.-II.Corinther 6:16.
Text for June 17, 1772.

145   GEISLER, JOHANN CHRISTIAN (1729-1815) *Zum 17. Aug. 1772*
       in Herrnhuth
       [Redet unter einander]

SSAB;Str;Harpa;fig.bass.-B-Flat maj.-72m.-Epheser 5:19,20; Hymn.
Text and Hymn for August 17, 1772.

146   HERBST, JOHANNES (1735-1812) *Zum 29. Aug. 1772*

146.1 [Lasset euch nicht]

SSAB;Str.-E maj.-*Moderato.*-57m.-Ebräer 13:9.
Losung for August 29, 1772.

146.2 [In allen Dingen]

SSAB;Str.-A maj.-*Andante.*-74m.-II.Corinther 6:4.
Text for August 29, 1772.

147   VERBEEK, JOHANN RENATUS (1748-1820) *Zum 29. Aug. 1772*

147.1 [In allen Dingen]

SATB;Str.-B-Flat maj.-*Allegretto.*-37m.-II.Corinther 6:4; Hymn.
Text for August 29, 1772.

147.2 [Lasset euch nicht]

S/SATB;Str.-G maj.-*Allegro.*-30m.-Ebräer 13:9.
Losung for August 29, 1772.

148a   GEISLER, JOHANN CHRISTIAN (1729-1815) *Zum 29. Aug. 1772*

148a[.1] [Wie wird ein Jüngling—Wenn er sich hält]

S"*recit acc*"/SSAB;Str.-D maj.-29m.-Psalm 119:1.
At end: "*Segue/Wende dich zu uns die deinen Namen lieben ex D dur.*"

148a[.2] [Lass unsern Gang]

SSAB;Str.-B min;D maj;A maj.-*Andante;Langsam.*-
70m.-Psalm 119:133,135,124,153,22,109,105.

148b   GEISLER, JOHANN CHRISTIAN (1729-1815) *Zum 7. Sept. 1772*
[Nun Herr Gott! bekräftige—Fahre fort]

SSAB;Str;keyboard.-D maj.-*Grave.*-64m.-II.Samuelis 7:25,26,29.
Alternate text incipit for second section: *Habe an. . .*

149   GEISLER, JOHANN CHRISTIAN (1729-1815) *Losung am 16. Oct. 1772*
[Israel wird sicher alleine]

SSAB;Str.-D maj.-*Moderato.*-104m.-V.Mose 33:28; Hymn.
Losung and Hymn for October 16, 1772.

150   GEISLER, JOHANN CHRISTIAN (1729-1815) *Zum 11. Dec. 1772*
[Wir gratuliren dir]

SS;2Fl;Str.-E-Flat maj.-*Langsam.*-49m.-Hymn.

151   GEISLER, JOHANN CHRISTIAN (1729-1815) *Zum 25. Mart. 1773*
[Eines ist Noth]

SSAB;Str;Harpa;Cembalo.-F maj.-49m.-Lucä 10:42.

152   GEISLER, JOHANN CHRISTIAN (1729-1815) *Zum grossen
Sabbath 1773*
[Ey das war eine schöne Leich]

S;Str;keyboard.-A min.-*Lento.*-40m.-Hymn.
Quotations from Hymn 153,6; Tune 151A.

153   HERBST, JOHANNES (1735-1812) *Zum grossen Sabbath
am 10. Apr. 1773*
[Gelobet sey der Herr, gross von Rath]

SSAB;Str.-B-Flat maj.-*Moderato.*-97m.-Jeremia 32:19; 33:9; Psalm 111:4;
Ebräor 7:27.
For an SATB version, see Herbst 153[b].

153[b]   HERBST, JOHANNES (1735-1812) *Zum grossen Sabbath
am 10. Apr. 1773*
[Gelobet sey der Herr, gross von Rath]

SATB;Str.-B-Flat maj.-*Moderato.*-97m.-Jeremia 32:19; 33:9;
Psalm 111:4;Ebräer 7:27.
For an SSAB version, see Herbst 153.

154   HERBST, JOHANNES (1735-1812) *Zum 4. May 1773*

154.1   [Ich gehe einher in der Kraft]

S;Str.-F maj.-*Andante.*-56m.-Psalm 71:16.
Losung for May 4, 1773.

154.2   [Weil ihr denn Kinder]

SATB;Str.-F maj.-*Larghetto.*-62m.-Galater 4:6.

155   GEISLER, JOHANN CHRISTIAN (1729-1815) *Zum 4. May 1773*

155.1   [Ich gehe einher in der Kraft]

SSAB;Str;Harpa.-F maj.-62m.-Psalm 71:6.
Losung for May 4, 1773.

155.2   [Weil ihr denn Kinder]

SSAB;Harpa;Str.-B-Flat maj.-*Andante.*-79m.-Galater 4:6.

156   GEHRA, AUGUST HEINRICH (1715-1785) *Zum 4. May, 1773*

156.1   [Wohl dem, den du erwehlest]

SSAB;Str;2 Harps.-G maj.-*Moderato.*-107m.-Psalm 65:5.

156.2   [Der Eindruck seiner Schmerzen]

SSAB;Clavecin;Harpa;Vla.obl;Vcl.obl.-G maj.-*Andante.*-72m.-Hymn.

157   GEISLER, JOHANN CHRISTIAN (1729-1815) *Zum 22. May 1773*
       [Ihr holden Töne]

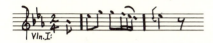

SS;Str;Harpa;Cembalo.-E-Flat maj.-*Gratioso.*-85m.-Hymn.

158[.1] HASSE, JOHANN ADOLPH (1699-1783) *Text am 8. July 1773*
       [Der gesegnete Kelch]

S;Str.-E-Flat maj.-*Adagio.*-70m.-I.Corinther 10:16,17.
Adapted from Hasse's *Sant' Elena,* Part II, No. 2: "Demirans hoc".
[See B XIV]

158[.2] HASSE, JOHANN ADOLPH (1699-1783) *Texte am 10. und 11.
       July 1773*
       [Unser Herr Jesus—So oft ihr]

SSAAB;2Fl;2Bn;Str;Fondamento.-E-Flat maj.-*Largo.*-125m.-
I.Corinther 11:23-26.
Adapted from Hasse's *I Pellegrini:* "Tu portas nobis." [See B XIII]
For another arr., see Herbst 158[.2b].
See also Herbst 161.1.

158[.2b]HASSE, JOHANN ADOLPH (1699-1783)
       [Unser Herr Jesus—So oft ihr]

SSAB;Str.-D maj.-*Lento.*-125m.-I.Corinther 11:23-26.
Adapted from Hasse's *I Pellegrini:* "Tu portas nobis." [See B XIII]
For another arr., see Herbst 158[.2].
See also Herbst 161.1.

159   HERBST, JOHANNES (1735-1812) *Zum 29. Aug. 1773*

159.1   [Gleichwie ein Mann]

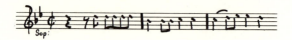

SATB;Str.-B-Flat maj.-*Andante.*-31m.-Jeremia 13:11.
Losung for August 29, 1773.
At end: *"Choral: Siehe hinten"*

159.2   [Ein jeglicher sey gesinnet]

S;Str.-F maj.-*Larghetto*-66m.-Philipper 2:5.
Text for August 29, 1773.

159[.3] [Freu dich, kleine Heerd!]

SATB.-B-Flat maj.-9m.-Hymn 950; Tune 5A.
Hymn for August 29, 1773.

160   GEISLER, JOHANN CHRISTIAN (1729-1815) *Zum 29. Aug. 1773*

160.1   [Gleichwie ein Mann—Freu dich, kleine Heerd!]

SSAB;Str.-F maj.-*Moderato.*-88m.-Jeremia 13:11; Hymn 950.
Losung and Hymn for August 29, 1773.

160.2   [Ein jeglicher sey gesinnet]

SSAB;Str.-B-Flat maj.-*Lento.*-25m.-Philipper 2:5.
Text for August 29, 1773.

161   HASSE, JOHANN ADOLPH (1699-1783) *Zum 29. Aug. 1773*

161.1   [Ja Dank- und Lobelieder]

SSAAB;Str.-F maj.-*Lento Con Sordini.*-116m.-Hymn.
Alternate texts: *Eilt wie Verlobte* and *Haupt deiner Kreuz-Gemeine*
Adapted from Hasse's *I Pellegrini*: "Tu portas nobis" [See B XIII]
See also Herbst 158[.2] and 158[.2b].

161.2   [Erheb, o Chor, erhebe das Herz]

SATB; Str.-F maj.-*Lento ma poco.*-104m.
Adapted from Hasse's *Converzione di St. Agostino*: "Inspira, o Deus."
[See B VIII]

162   GEISLER, JOHANN CHRISTIAN (1729-1815) *Zum 7. Septembr. 1773*
      [Ich will singen von der Gnade—So krieget Jesus]

SSAB;Str.-F maj.-*Poco allegro.*-98m.-Psalm 89:2;
Hymn 1044,9 (Zinzendorf).

163   GEISLER, JOHANN CHRISTIAN (1729-1815) *Zum 24. Dec. 1773*
      [Der Herr ist kommen]

SSAB;Str.-G maj.-*Munter.*-58m.-II. Samuelis 22:10.

164   GEISLER, CHRISTIAN GOTTFRIED (1730-1810) *Zum grossen
      Sabbath d. 2. Apr. 1774*

164.1   [Er neigte Sein Haupt—O die Minut]

SSAB;Str.-C min.-108m.-Johannis 19:30; Hymn 175, 4, 5
(C. R. v. Zinzendorf), var; Tune 14B.

164.2   [Wohlan! Ich will meinem Lieben]

SS/SSAB;Str.-E-Flat maj;C min.-*Langsam.*-76m.-Jesaia 5:1;
Hymn; Tune 151A.

164.3   [Ich denke der vorigen Tage]

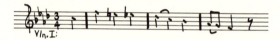

SSAB;Str.-F min.-*Langsam. mit Sordinen.*-68m.-Jesaia 53:5;
Klaglieder 1:12.

164.4   [Siehe, das ist Gottes Lamm—Fürwahr Er trug unsre Krankheit]
Sehet, das ist Gottes Lamm

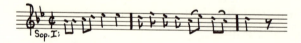

SSAB/SSAB;Str.-B-Flat maj.-*Langsam.*-74m.-Johannis 1:29;
Jesaia 53:3-5.
Contains excerpts from Karl Heinrich Graun's *Siehe, das ist Gottes
Lamm* [Herbst 104.2]

164.5   [Kommet her und sehet]

SSAB;Str.-C min.-*Langsam.*-50m.-Matthäi 28:6; Hymn.

165   HERBST, JOHANNES (1735-1812) *Zum 4. May 1774*

165.1   [Singt dem Herrn ein neues Lied. Lobet]

SATB.-E-Flat maj.-15m.-Tune 119,var.

165.2   [Wie theuer ist deine Güte]

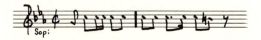

SATB.-C min.-*Larghetto.*-29m.-Psalm 36:8.
Adapted from J. A. Hasse's *Giuseppe Liberato*: "Defende populum tuum." [See B XI]
For another version, see Herbst 283.

165.3   [Die gepflanzt sind in dem Hause]

SATB;Su.-C maj.-*Andante.*-62m.-Psalm 92:14,15.
Losung for May 4, 1774.

165.4   [Gott ists, der uns bevestigt]

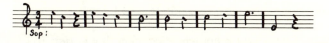

SATB;Str.-A min.-*Munter, doch nicht zu geschwind.*-77m.-
II.Corinther 1:21,22.
Text for May 4, 1774.
At end: Tune 149A, melody and fig. bass.

166   GEISLER, JOHANN CHRISTIAN (1729-1815) *Zum 4. May 1774*

166.1   [Die gepflanzt sind in dem Hause]

SSAB;Str.-F maj.-*Andante moderato.*-74m.-Psalm 92:14,15.
Losung for May 4, 1774.

166.2 [Gott ists, der uns bevestigt]

SSAB;Str.-B-Flat maj.-39m.-II.Corinther 1:21,22.
Text for May 4, 1774.

167 GEISLER, JOHANN CHRISTIAN (1729-1815) *Zum Pfingst-Fest d. 22. May 1774*

167.1 [Ich will meinen Geist]

S;Str.-G maj.-*Larghetto.*-48m.-Joel 3:1.
At end: "*Gem. Es sollen die Unmündigen;/Komm Heiliger Geist Herre Gott* [Hymn 294]."

167.2 [Wenn der Geist der Wahrheit]

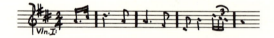

S;Str.-D maj.-*Lento.*-58m.-Johannis 16:13,14.
Text for May 22, 1774.
At end: "*Gem. Und ich bin sein Kind, dem Aug u. Herz;/Du heiliges Licht, edler Hort* [Hymn 294,2]."

167.3 [Sein Geist hilft unsrer Schwachheit]
Coro.

SSAB;Str.-*Molto Andante.*-91m.-Römer 8:26.

168 HERBST, JOHANNES (1735-1812) *Zum 29. Aug. 1774*
[Halt an dem Vorbilde]

SATB;Str.-F maj.-*Andante.*-107m.-II.Timotheum 1:13,14.
Text for August 29, 1774.

169   VERBEEK, JOHANN RENATUS (1748-1820) *Zum 29. Aug. 1774*

169[.1] [Halt an dem Vorbilde]

S;Str.-G maj;B-Flat maj.-*Arioso.*-59m.-II.Timotheum 1:13,14.
Text for August 29, 1774.

169[.2] [Ein jeglicher sey gesinnet]

SATB;Str.-G maj.-*Poco Lento.*-23m.-Philipper 2:5.

170.1   GEISLER, JOHANN CHRISTIAN (1729 1815) *Zum 29. Aug. 1774*
        [Vor dir ist Freude]

SSAB;Str. C maj.-*Vivace.*-99m.-Psalm 16:11.
Losung for August 29, 1774.

170.2   HASSE, JOHANN ADOLPH (1699-1783) *Zum 29. Aug. 1774*
        [Lob sey dir, Gott unser Heiland]
        Coro.

SSATB;Str.-C maj.-152m.
Adapted from Hasse's *La Caduta di Gerico,* no. 1: "A te lode eterne."
[See B X]

171   GEISLER, JOHANN CHRISTIAN (1729-1815)
       Zum Witwer-fest d. 31. Aug. 1774

171.1   [Singet Ihm, lobsinget]

SSAB;Str.-D maj.-*Allegro Moderato.*-60m.-Psalms 68:5,6; 145:14;
140:13; 68:6; 4:2; Hiob 24:21.
See also Herbst 190b.

171.2   [In der Angst rief ich]

SSAB;Str.-B min.-*Largo.*-71m.-Psalm 118:5.
Losung for August 31, 1774.

172   HERBST, JOHANNES (1735-1812) *Zum grossen Sabbath 1775*
       [Fürwahr, Er trug unsre Krankheit]

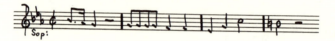

SATB;Str.-E-Flat maj.-*Langsam.*-56m.-Jesaia 53:4,5.
See also Herbst 290.2 and Herbst 393.

173   HERBST, JOHANNES (1735-1812) *Zum 4. May 1775*

173.1   [Das Land ist voll Erkenntniss]

SATB;Str.-B-Flat maj.-*Lebhaft.*-55m.-Jesaia 11:9.
Losung for May 4, 1775.

173.2   [Bleibet in mir]

S;Str.-F maj.-*Angenehm u. zärtlich.*-76m.-Johannis 15:4.
Text for May 4, 1775.

174   GEISLER, JOHANN CHRISTIAN (1729-1815) *Zum 4. May 1775*

174.1   [Das Land ist voll Erkenntniss—Und wenn die Wundenfluthen]

SSAB;Str.-B-Flat maj;E-Flat maj.-73m.-Jesaia 11:9; Hymn.
Losung for May 4, 1775.

174.2   [Bleibet in mir]

S;Str.-B-Flat maj.-*Lento.*-32m.-Johannis 15:4.
Text for May 4, 1775.

174.3   [Gnade und Friede sey über euch]

SSAB.-B-Flat maj.-22m.

175   GEISLER, JOHANN CHRISTIAN (1729-1815) *Zur Eröffnung des
        Synodi d. 1. July, 1775*
        [Die Herrlichkeit des Herrn]

SSAB;Str.-E-Flat maj.-*Grave.*-49m.-Jesaia 40:5.

176   HERBST, JOHANNES (1735-1812) *Zum 29. Aug. 1775*
        [Gott der Herr ist meine Stärke]

SATB;Str.-C maj.-*Lebhaft.*-50m.-Psalm 118:14.
Losung for August 29, 1775.

177   GEISLER, JOHANN CHRISTIAN (1729-1815) *Text zum 29. Aug. 1775*
[So ihr bleiben]

S;Fl;Str.-C maj.-38m.-Johannis 8:31,32.
See also Herbst 177b.

[177b] GEISLER, JOHANN CHRISTIAN (1729-1815) *Text zum 29. Aug. 1775*
[So ihr bleiben]

S;Fl;Str.-A maj.-38m.-Johannis 8:31,32.
See also Herbst 177.

178   VERBEEK, JOHANN RENATUS (1748-1820) *Zum 24. Dec. 1775*
[Uns ist ein Kind geboren]

SATB;2Fl;[2Hns];Str;fig.bass.-C maj.-*Allegro moderato.*-
125m.-Jesaia 9:6.
Horn pts. on separate sheet.

179   HERBST, JOHANNES (1735-1812) *Zum 4. May 1776*

179.1   [Du solst erfahren]

S;Str.-D maj.-*Andante.*-89m.-Jesaia 60:16.
Losung for May 4, 1776.

179.2 [Ihr habt mich nicht erwehlet]

S;Str.-F maj.-*Affettuoso.*-84m.-Johannis 15:16.
Text for May 4, 1776.

179.3 [Das Lamm das erwürget ist]

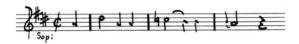

SATB;Str.-D maj.-*Andante, mit Affect.*-53m.-Offenbarung 5:12.

180 HERBST, JOHANNES (1735-1812) *Zum 29. Aug. 1776*
[Lobsinget dem Herrn]

SATB;[2Hns];Str.-C maj.-*Munter.*-49m.-Jesaia 12:5.
Losung for August 29, 1776.
Horn pts. on separate sheet.

181 VERBEEK, JOHANN RENATUS (1748-1820) *Zum 29. Aug. 1776*
[Lobsinget dem Herrn]
missing

182 HERBST, JOHANNES (1735-1812) *Zum 31. Aug. 1776*
[Wo euer Schatz ist]

SS;Str.-G maj.-*Angenehm.*-61m.-Matthäi 6:21.
Text for August 31, 1776.

183   HERBST, JOHANNES (1735-1812) *Zum 7. Sept. 1776*
[Ich bin der Herr]

SATB;Str.-B-Flat maj.-*Bedächtig.*-31m.-Jesaia 45:19.
Losung for September 7, 1776.

184   HERBST, JOHANNES (1735-1812) *Zum 4. May 1777*

184.1   [Ich will euch wie ein Thau]

SATB;Str.-G maj.-*Lieblich.*-64m.-Hosea 14:6.

184.2   [Sie sollen über Seinen Name]

SATB;Str.-D maj.-*Munter, doch nicht zu geschwinde.*-69m.-Psalm 89:17.

184.3   [Es ist in keinem andern Heil]

SATB;Str.-G maj.-*Bedachtsam.*-95m.-Apostelgeschichte 4:12.
Losung for May 4, 1777.

184.4   [Bleibet in Seiner Liebe]

SS;Str.-A maj.-*Angenehm.*-121m.-Johannis 15:9-11.

184.5 [Unser keiner lebt ihm selber]

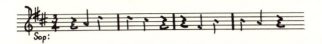

SATB;Str.-D maj.-*Andante.*-71m.-Römer 14:7,8; Hymn.
Alternate setting from m.35 on separate sheet.

185 GEISLER, JOHANN CHRISTIAN (1729-1815) *Zum 4. May 1777*
[Es ist in keinem andern Heil]

SSAB;Str.-A maj.-*Moderato.*-72m.-Apostelgeschichte 4:12.
Losung for May 4, 1777.

186 GEISLER, JOHANN CHRISTIAN (1729-1815) *Die Losung zum
29. August 1777*
[Das Wort des Herrn—Sein Wort läuft]

SSAB;Str.-E-Flat maj.-93m.-Apostelgeschichte 19:20; Hymn.

187 HERBST, JOHANNES (1735-1812) *Zum 29. Aug. 1777*
[Dis ist ein Tag]

SS;Str.-G maj.-*Frölich.*-81m.-Psalm 118:24.

188 CRUSE, [G. D.?(fl. 1777] *Zum 29. Aug. 1777*

188[.1] [Das Wort des Herrn]

SATB;2Fl;2Hns;Str.-D maj.-*Allegro Maestoso.*-47m.-
Apostelgeschichte 19:20.
Losung for August 29, 1777.

188[.2] [Dis ist ein Tag]

SATB;2Fl;Str.-D maj.-*Allegro, un poco Vivace.*-42m.-Psalm 118:24.

188[.3] [Nun der Gott des Friedens]

SATB;2Fl;Str.-A maj.-*Andante con Giusto.*-78m.-
I.Thessalonicher 5:23.

189   HERBST, JOHANNES (1735-1812) *Zum 31. Aug. 1777*

189.1   [Wir segnen euch]

SATB;Str.-F maj.-*Andante.*-44m.-Psalm 118:26.

189.2   [Ihr seyd das auserwehlte Geschlecht]

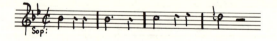

SATB;Str.-B-Flat maj.-*Moderato.*-58m.-I.Petri 2:9.
Losung for August 31, 1777.

189b   GEISLER, JOHANN CHRISTIAN (1729-1815) *Losung zum 31.*
        Aug. 1777
        [Ihr seyd das auserwehlte Geschlecht]

SSAB;Str.-E-Flat maj.-*Largo.*-34m.-I.Petri 2:9.

190   HERBST, JOHANNES (1735-1812) *Zum 7. Sept. 1777*
[Danket dem Herrn, denn Er ist]

SATB;[2Hns];Str.-D maj.-*Munter.*-78m.-I.Chronica 17:34.
Horn pts. on separate sheet.

190b   GEISLER, JOHANN CHRISTIAN (1729-1815) *Zum 7. Sept. 1777*
[Danket dem Herrn, denn Er ist]

SSAB;2Fl;Str.-D maj.-*Allegro moderato.*-52m.-I.Chronica 17:34.
See also Herbst 171.1.

191   VERBEEK, JOHANN RENATUS (1748-1820) *Zum 24. Dec. 1777*
[Siehe, das ist unser Gott]

SSTB;Str;keyboard;fig.bass.-A maj.-*Andante.*-48m.-Jesaia 25:9.

192   GRAUN, KARL HEINRICH (1701-1759) and JOHANN RENATUS
VERBEEK (1748-1820) *Zum grossen Sabbath 1778*

192.1   [Er war der allerverachteste] by Graun

SATB;Str.-A min.-*Larghetto.*-36m.-Jesaia 53:3.
From his *Passions-Cantate.*

192.2   [Nun soll Er seine Lust] by Verbeek

SATB;Str.-A maj.-*Largo.*-68m.-Jesaia 53:11,12.
For another version, see Herbst 193.

193   VERBEEK, JOHANN RENATUS (1748-1820)
        [Nun soll Er seine Lust]

SATB/SSA;2 Vcl;Str.-A maj.-*Largo.*-68m.-Jesaia 53:11,12.
For another version, see Herbst 192.2.

194   GEISLER, JOHANN CHRISTIAN (1729-1815) *Zum 4. May 1778*

194.1   [Gelobet sey der Herr, der unser Gebet]

SSAB;2Fl;Str.-D maj.-*Allegro moderato.*-53m.-Psalm 66:20.

194.2   [Herzlich lieb habe ich dich]

SSAB;2Fl;Str.-A maj.-*Affettuoso.*-72m.-Psalm 18:2.
At beginning: *"Wenn die Flöten dazu gespielt werden ob werden die
Viol. ripien. gespielt u. die andern Violinen bleiben weg."*

194.3   [So thut nun Fleiss]

SSAB;2Fl;Str.-D maj.-*Moderato.*-81m.-II. Petri 3:14.
Text for May 4, 1778.

195   HERBST, JOHANNES (1735-1812) *Zum 4. May 1778*

195.1   [Gelobet sey der Herr, der unser Gebet]

SATB;Str.-A maj.-*Munter, doch nicht zu geschwind.*-88m.-Psalm 66:20.

195.2   [Herzlich lieb habe ich dich]

SATB;Str.-E maj.-*Affettuoso.*-63m.-Psalm 18:2.

195.3   [So thut nun Fleiss]

SATB;Str.-D maj.-*Andante.*-105m.-II.Petri 3:14.
Text for May 4, 1778.

196   HERBST, JOHANNES (1735-1812) *Zum 29. Aug. 1778*

196.1   [Wenn du Ihn anriefst]

SATB;Str.-D min.-*Lento.*-71m.-Psalm 120:1.

196.2   [Ich danke dir ewiglich]

SATB;Str.-F maj.-*Andante.*-77m.-Psalm 52:11.
Losung for August 29, 1778.

197   FREYDT, JOHANN LUDWIG (1748-1807) *Zum 29. Aug. 1778*

197[.1] [Du Herr Gott bist barmherzig]

S/SSAB;Str.-F maj.-*Andante.*-60m.-Psalm 86:15.

197[.2] [Ich danke dir ewiglich]

SSAB;Str.-Cmaj.-*Mittelmässig geschwind.*-102m.-Psalm 52:11.
Losung for August 29, 1778.

198 GEISLER, JOHANN CHRISTIAN (1729-1815) *Zum 31. Aug. 1778*
[Gott hat uns angenehm]

SSAB;2Fl;Str.-D maj.-*Andante.*-92m.-Epheser 1:6,7.
Text for August 31, 1778.

199 FREYDT, JOHANN LUDWIG (1748-1807) *Zum 31. Aug. 1778*
[Gott hat uns angenehm]

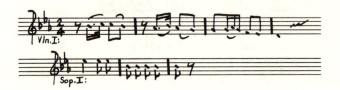

SSAB;Str.-E-Flat maj.-*Langsam.*-84m.-Epheser 1:6,7.
Text for August 31, 1778.

200 WANHAL, JOHANN BAPTIST (1739-1813) *Zum 7. Sept. 1778*
[Singt und spielt] *missing*
Alternate text: *Schönstes Kind*

201.1 FREYDT, JOHANN LUDWIG (1748-1807) *Zum 13. Nov. 1778*
[Herr und Aeltster deiner Kreuzgemeine]

SSAB;Str.-F maj.-*Langsam.*-81m.-Hymn 1109,1 (Zinzendorf).
P.1 crossed out, with note: "*Vide auf einem besondern Blat*
No. 201b."

201.1b FREYDT, JOHANN LUDWIG (1748-1807) *Zum 13. Nov. 1778*
[Herr und Aeltster deiner Kreuzgemeine]

SSAB;Str;fig.bass.-F maj.-*Langsam.*-81m.-Hymn 1109, 1 (Zinzendorf).

201[.2] FREYDT, JOHANN LUDWIG (1748-1807) *Zum 29. Aug. 1778*
[Wenn du Ihn anriefst]

SSAB;Str.-C maj.-*Mittelmässig.*-71m.-Psalm 120:1.

201[.3] FREYDT, JOHANN LUDWIG (1748-1807) *Zum 24. Dec. 1778*
[Das Wort ward Fleisch]

SSAB;Str.-E-Flat maj.-*Etwas munter.*-51m.-Johannis 1:14.
For a different version, see Herbst 296.1.

202   FREYDT, JOHANN LUDWIG (1748-1807) *Zum Knaben-fest 1779*
      [Das ist je gewisslich wahr]

SSAB;Str.-E-Flat maj.-*Mässig.*-125m.-I.Timotheum 1:15.

203   FREYDT, JOHANN LUDWIG (1748-1807) *Zum 22. Merz als am*
      Tage der Einweihung des Anstalt Hauses in Niesky, 1779

203[.1]   [Gesegnet wirst du seyn]

SSAB;Str.-F maj.-*Langsam.*-93m.-V.Mose 28:6.

203[.2]   [So spricht der Herr: Sie sollen mich]

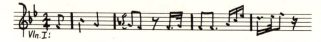

SSAB;Str.-B-Flat maj.-*Lebhaft.*-56m.-Jeremia 31:34.

203[.3]   [Siehe alle diese kommen]

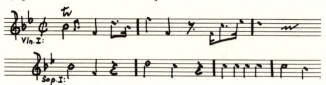

SSAB;Str.-B-Flat maj.-*Grave.*-54m.-Jesaia 49:18.

204   ROLLE, JOHANN HEINRICH (1718-1785) *Zum gr. Sabbath 1779*
      [Mein Heiland geht ins Leiden]

S;2Fl;Str[keyboard].-A min.-*Poco Largo e Cantabile.*-78m.-Hymn.
Alternate texts: *Wie Jesu Geist am Ende* and *Gleichwie ein milder*
Regen.
Instrumental introduction contains keyboard sketch.
See Herbst 204.1.

204.1   ROLLE, JOHANN HEINRICH (1718-1785) *Zum gr. Sabbath 1779*
        [Mein Heiland geht ins Leiden]

S;2Fl;Str.-A min.-*Poco Largo e Cantabile.*-78m.-Hymn.
Alternate text: *Wie Jesu Geist am Ende.*
See Herbst 204.

204.2 HANDEL, GEORGE FREDERICK (1685-1759)
[In meines Herren Tod]

SS;2Bn;Str.-F maj.-*Largo.*-39m.-Hymns 175,1,2; 606,1,2(C. R. v.
Zinzendorf).

205 HERBST, JOHANNES (1735-1812) *Zum 4. May 1779*
[So spricht der Herr Zebaoth—Das ist unbeschreiblich]

T/SATB;Str.-F maj.-*Mit Affect u. lieblich.*-88m.-Sacharja 2:8;
Hymn 756 (Zinzendorf).
Losung and Hymn for May 4, 1779.

206 GEISLER, JOHANN CHRISTIAN (1729-1815) *Zum 4. May 1779*
[So spricht der Herr Zebaoth—Das ist unbeschreiblich]

B/SSAB;Str.-D maj.-*Andante.*-133m.-Sacharja 2:8; Hymn 756
(Zinzendorf).
Losung and Hymn for May 4, 1779.

207 FREYDT, JOHANN LUDWIG (1748-1807) *Zum 4ten May 1779*
[So spricht der Herr Zebaoth–Das ist unbeschreiblich]

SSAB;Str.-F maj.-*Maestoso;Mittelmässig geschwinder.*-111m.-
Sacharja 2:8; Hymn 756 (Zinzendorf).
Losung and Hymn for May 4, 1779.

208 FREYDT, JOHANN LUDWIG (1748-1807) *Zum 8. Aug. 1779*

208.1 [Die Gemeine hatte Friede]

SSAB;Str.-C maj.-*Moderato.*-52m.-Apostelgeschichte 9:31.

208.2 [Dis Volk habe ich]

S;Str.-C min.-39m.-Jesaia 43:21.
Losung for August 8, 1779.

208.3 [Ihm sey Ehre]

SSAB;Str.-C maj.-*Erhaben.*-17m.-Epheser 3:21.

208.4 [Gott dein Stuhl bleibt]

B/SSAB;Str.-D maj.-*Freudig.*-47m.-Psalm 45:7.

209   HERBST, JOHANNES (1735-1812) *Zum 29. Aug. 1779*
[Höret alle die ihr—Deine Missethat]

SATB;Str.-E-Flat maj.-*Lento;Munterer.*-143m.-Jesaia 57:15;
Klaglieder 4:22; Hymn 1830 [Kl. Br. Ges.].
Losung and Hymn for August 29, 1779.

210   GEISLER, JOHANN CHRISTIAN (1729-1815) *Zum 29. Aug. 1779*
[Höret alle die ihr—Deine Missethat]

S/SSAB;Str.-D maj.-*Andante.*-101m.-Jesaia 57:15; Klaglieder 4:22;
Hymn 1830 [Kl. Br. Ges.].
Losung and Hymn for August 29, 1779.

211   FREYDT, JOHANN LUDWIG (1748-1807) *Zum 29. Aug. 1779*
[Höret alle die ihr—Deine Missethat]

B/SSAB;Str.-B min;B maj.-*Grave; Andante.*-69m.-Jesaia 57:15;
Klaglieder 4:22; Hymn 1830 [Kl. Br. Ges.].
Losung and Hymn for August 29, 1779.

212   GEISLER, JOHANN CHRISTIAN (1729-1815) *Zum 7. Septembr. 1779*

212.1   [Die Gnade des Herrn Jesu Christ]

SSB;2Fl;Str.-D maj.-33m.-Hymn 260 (Watteville), var.

212.2   [Er wird es thun]

SSB;2Fl;Str.-G maj.-34m.-Hymn.

212.3   [Er hat uns aus der Welt]

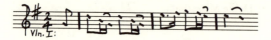

SSB;2Fl;Str.-G maj.-28m.-Hymn.

212.4   [Wohl dir, o Chor]

SSB;2Fl;Str.-D maj.-27m.-Hymn.

212.5   [Er, der dich Ihm]

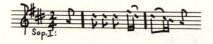

SSAB;2Fl;Str.-D maj.-19m.-Hymn.

213.1   FREYDT, JOHANN LUDWIG (1748-1807) *Zum 7. Sept. 1779*
         [Er, der dich Ihm]
         Aria

S;Str.-A min.-*Andantino.*-43m.-Hymn.

213.2   FREYDT, JOHANN LUDWIG (1748-1807) *Zum 13. Nov. 1779*
[Wo ist ein solcher Freund—Freue dich, o Gemeine]
Coro.

S;Str/SSAB;Str.-D maj.-*Andante;Allegretto.*-85m.
See Herbst 213.2b.

213.3   [Alle Gottes-Verheissungen—Was Er verspricht]

SSAB;Str.-D maj.-*Moderato;Andante.*-62m.-II.Corinther 1:20;
Hymn 231,3 (Freylinghausen).
Text and Hymn for November 13, 1779.

213.2b   [Wo ist ein solcher Freund—Freue dich, o Gemeine]

S;Str/SSAB;Str.-D maj.-*Andantino;Poco Allegro.*-81m.
See Herbst 213.2.

214a   FREYDT, JOHANN LUDWIG (1748-1807) *Zum 25. Dec. 1779*
[Vor dir wird man—Die Engel und Menschen]

S/SSAB:Str.-C maj.-*Vivace.*-129m.-Jesaia 9:3; Hymn.
Losung and Hymn for December 25, 1779.
For another version, see Herbst 214b.

214b   FREYDT, JOHANN LUDWIG (1748-1807) *Zum 13. Dec. 1779*
        [Vor dir wird man—Die Engel und Menschen]

SSAB;2Hns[or Trpt];Str;Vcl;Organo(fig.bass).-C maj.-*Vivace.-*
135m.-Jesaia 9:3;Hymn.
For another version, see Herbst 214a.

214b[.2]ROLLE, JOHANN HEINRICH (1718-1785) *Zum 24. Decembr. 1778*
        [Lobt den Herrn! die Gnadensonne]

SATB;Str.-E-Flat maj.-69m.-Hymn.
Alternate text: *Lobt den Herrn, den Geist der Gnaden ["Zu Pfingsten"]*
See Herbst [98b.1]

215   GRIMM, JOHANN DANIEL (1719-1760) *Zu Weynachten*
        [Der ist von Gott geboren]
        Arietta

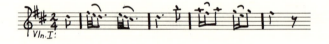

S;2Trpt;Str.-D maj.-*Vivace.-*69m.-Hymn.

216   GRIMM, JOHANN DANIEL (1719-1760)
        [Wenn ich so alleine]

SS;Str.-D min.-*Andante.-*52m.-Hymn 176,3 (C. R. v. Zinzendorf).
Alternate text: *Selge Lebenstunden* [Hymn 1711 (Loskiel)].

217.1   BRUININGK, HEINRICH VON (1738-1785)
        [Hört im Geist ihr Hallelujah]

S;Str.-C maj.-70m.-Hymn.
Alternate text: *Helft doch heilig Tönen.*

217.2   SCHLICHT, LUDOLPH ERNST (1714-1769)
        [Was ist Er dir dann?]

S;Str.-G maj.-14m.-Hymn.

217.3   GEISLER, JOHANN CHRISTIAN (1729-1815)
        [Siehe da ein Hütte Gottes]

SS;Str.-G maj.-48m.-Offenbarung 21:3; Psalm 84:2; Sprüche 8:31;
Jesaia 57:15.
Derived from Christian Gregor's setting (Herbst 14.8).

217.4   GEISLER, JOHANN CHRISTIAN (1729-1815)
        [Das ist der grosse Zweck]

SS;Str.-C maj.-36m.-Hymn.

217.5   [UNIDENTIFIED]
        [Mein Geist mit Taubenflügeln]

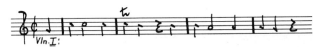

SS;Str.-C maj.-37m.-Hymn.

218   HASSE, JOHANN ADOLPH (1699-1783)
        [O Lamm Gottes unschuldig]

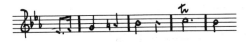

Hymn 126 (Decius); Tune 127, var.
Cembalo pt. only (with text).
From his *Sant Elena al Calvario.* [See B XIV]

219   BACH, CARL PHILLIPP EMANUEL (1714-1788)
       [Kommt lasset uns anbeten]
       Motetta

SATB;2Ob;Str;fig. bass-A min;C maj.-*Poco Largo.*-29m.-Psalm 95:6.
Alternate text: O come, let us worship.

220[.1] GEISLER, JOHANN CHRISTIAN (1729-1815)
        [Ihr seyd die Gesegneten]

SSAB;Str.-D maj.-*Larghetto.*-64m.-Psalm 115:15.

220[.2] GEISLER, JOHANN CHRISTIAN (1729-1815)
        [Der Herr hat des Tages]

SSAB;Str.-A maj.-*Allegro.*-84m.-Psalm 42:9.

221   GEISLER, JOHANN CHRISTIAN (1729-1815)
       [Der König wende sein Angesicht]

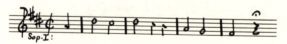

SSSAB;Str.-D maj.-*Langsam.*-29m.-II.Chronica 6:3.

222a   GEISLER, JOHANN CHRISTIAN (1729-1815)
       [Gott sey dir gnädig und segne]

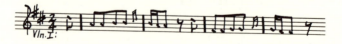

SSAB;keyboard;Str.-D maj.-43m.-Psalm 67:2;Philipper 4:9.

222b.1 GEISLER, JOHANN CHRISTIAN (1729-1815)
[Gott sey dir gnädig und segne—Der Gott des Friedens]

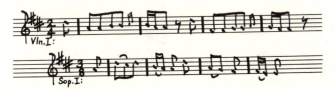

SS;Str.-D maj.-*Langsam.*-66m.-Psalm 67:2;Philipper 4:9.
Alternate text for last section: *Und bewahr uns.*
SSAB vocal score on separate sheet.

222b.2 GEISLER, JOHANN CHRISTIAN (1729-1815)
[Verlasse uns nicht]

SS;Str.-C maj.-43m.-I.Königen 8:57,58.

223 GEISLER, JOHANN CHRISTIAN (1729-1815)
[Es segne dich Gott]

SSAB;Str.-F maj.-118m.-Hymn 1089, 1-3 (Zinzendorf).

224.1 HERBST, JOHANNES (1735-1812)
[Es müsse Friede seyn]

SSAB;Str.-G maj.-*Moderato.*-112m.-Psalm 122:7

224.2 ?HERBST, JOHANNES (1735-1812)
[Selig sind die Todten]

SSAB;Str.-G maj.-*Andante, semper piano. con Sordini.*-76m.-
Offenbarung 14:13.

224.3 GRIMM, JOHANN DANIEL (1719-1760)
[O welch angenehmer Schlummer]

S;Str.-A min.-*Soave. con Sordini.*-30m.-Hymn.
From his cantata, *Sie flochten eine Dornen Crone.*

225.1 GEHRA, AUGUST HEINRICH (1715-1785)
[Selig sind, die zu dem Abendmahl]

SSAB;Str.-D maj.-*Andante.*-47m.-Offenbarung 19:9.

225.2 GEISLER, JOHANN CHRISTIAN (1729-1815)
[Ich weiss das mein Erlöser lebt]

SS/SSAB;Str.-F maj.-*Moderato.*-68m.-Hiob 19:25,27.
Derived from Handel's *The Messiah*: "I know that my Redeemer liveth."

225.3 GEISLER, JOHANN CHRISTIAN (1729-1815)
[Gott hat uns erwählet]

SSAB;Str.-F maj.-*Andante.*-88m.-Epheser 1:4.

226.1 GEHRA, AUGUST HEINRICH (1715-1785)
[Das Loos ist dir gefallen—O welch ein immerwährend Fest]

SS;Str.-C maj.-*Lebhaft.*-33m.-Psalm 16:6; Hymn 452,11 (Zinzendorf); Tune 14A.

226.2 GEHRÀ, AUGUST HEINRICH (1715-1785)
[Dieser Tag is ein Tag]

SS;Str.-G maj.-*Andante molto.*-82m.-II. Königen 7:9; Psalm 65:12; V. Mose 28:8.

227 PERGOLESI, GIOVANNI BATTISTA (1710-1736) *Zum Erndtefest in Neudietendorf*

227[.1] [Jauchzet Gott alle Lande]

SSATB;2Trpts;2Hns;Str;fig.bass.-G maj.-69m.-Psalms 66:1,2; 65:10; 100:5; 65:2.
Derived from his *Missa:* "Gloria in excelsis" [See B XXVIII]

227[.2] [Gross sind die Werke]

SSATB;Str;fig.bass.-C maj.-*Largo;Presto.*-60m.-Psalm 111:2; Psalm 66:4,8.
Derived from his *Missa:* "Gratias agimus te." [See B XXVIII]

228 GEISLER, JOHANN CHRISTIAN (1729-1815)
[Meine Leiche Jesu]

SS;Str;Cembalo/SS;Str;Cembalo "*in 2 Chören.*"-F maj.-*Lento.*-74m.-Hymn 161,1 (Zinzendorf).
For another version, see Herbst [228a].

[228a] GEISLER, JOHANN CHRISTIAN (1729-1815)
        [Meine Leiche Jesu]

SS/SS;Str.-F maj.-*Lento.*-74m.-Hymn 161,1 (Zinzendorf).
For another version, see Herbst 228.

229 VERBEEK, JOHANN RENATUS (1748-1820)
     [Siehe, es kommt die Zeit]

SATB;Str.-F maj.-*Allegro moderato.*-61m.-Jeremia 23:5.

230 VERBEEK, JOHANN RENATUS (1748-1820)
     [Lass sich freuen]

SATB;Str.-B-Flat maj.-*Allegro.*-144m.-Psalm 5:12.

231[.1] FREYDT, JOHANN LUDWIG (1748-1807)
         [Opfer und Gaben]

SSAB;Str.-B-Flat maj.-*Nicht zu langsam.*-60m.-Ebräer 10:5;
Colosser 1:20.

231[.2] FREYDT, JOHANN LUDWIG (1748-1807)
         [Danket dem Herrn denn Er ist]

SSAB;Str.-C maj.-*Lebhaft.*-119m.-I.Chronica 17:34.

232   FREYDT, JOHANN LUDWIG (1748-1807)
[Nun ruht Er]

SSAB;Str.-F min.-*Langsam Cantabile.*-17m.-II.Mose 16:23;
Jesaia 11:10.

233.1   FREYDT, JOHANN LUDWIG (1748-1807)
[Lobet Gott den Herrn]

SSAB;Str;Organ.-E-Flat maj.-*Etwas munter.*-103m.-Psalm 26:5.

233.2   FREYDT, JOHANN LUDWIG (1748-1807)
[Alles was Othem hat—Ach wär ein jeder Puls]

SSAB;2Hns;Str.-F maj.-*Mittelmassig geschwind;Andante.*-
148m.-Psalm 150:6; Hymn 1376,2 (Zinzendorf).
See also Herbst 317.2.

234.1   FREYDT, JOHANN LUDWIG (1748-1807)
[Preise Jerusalem den Herrn]

SSAB;2 Trpts *"clarino"*;Str.-D maj.-*Munter u. freudig.*-
93m.-Psalm 147:12-14.

234.2   FREYDT, JOHANN LUDWIG (1748-1807)
[Gelobet sey der Herr, der Seinen Volke]

SSAB;2Trpt"*clarino*";Str.-D maj.-*Munter u. lebhaft.*-56m.-
I.Chronica 24:25.

235.1   FREYDT, JOHANN LUDWIG (1748-1807)
[Lieblichkeiten, die nicht aus]

S;Bn;Str.-B-Flat maj.-*Langsam.*-106m.-Hymn 166,9
(C. R. v. Zinzendorf).
A second copy marked "*Aria. Ao. 1779.*"

235.2   FREYDT, JOHANN LUDWIG (1748-1807)
[Ich bin der Hirte]

S;Str.-D min.-*Pastorale.Langsam.*-85m.-Johannis 10:2-4,15,27,28.

235.3   FREYDT, JOHANN LUDWIG (1748-1807)
[Das Loos ist mir gefallen]

S;Str.-F maj.-*Langsam.*-52m.-Psalm 16:6.

236.1   FREYDT, JOHANN LUDWIG (1748-1807)
[Wiederholts mit süssen Tönen]

S;Bn;Str.-B-Flat maj.-*Langsam u. gelassen.*-109m.-Hymn 122,1 (Gregor).

236.2   FREYDT, JOHANN LUDWIG (1748-1807)
[Meine Leiche Jesu]
Duetto

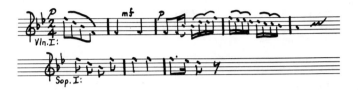

SS;Str.B-Flat maj.-*Langsam.*-75m.-Hymn 161,1 (Zinzendorf).

236.2b   FREYDT, JOHANN LUDWIG (1748-1807) *Zum grossen Sabbath 1778*
[Meine Leiche Jesu]
No. 4. Duetto

SS;Str;Organo(fig.bass).-B-Flat maj.-*Adagio.*-75m.-Hymn 161,1
(Zinzendorf).

236.3   FREYDT, JOHANN LUDWIG (1748-1807)
[So spricht der Herr: Dis Volk habe ich]

S;Str.-B-Flat maj.-*Andante.*-43m.-Jesaia 43:21; Jeremia 29:11.

236.4   FREYDT, JOHANN LUDWIG (1748-1807)
[Ich seh, ich seh mit Haufen]

SS;Str.-G min.-*Langsam.*-76m.-Hymn 63 [Kl. Br. Ges., III].
For another version, see Herbst 236.4b.

236.4b FREYDT, JOHANN LUDWIG (1748-1807) *Ao. 1779*
[Ich seh, ich seh mit Haufen]
Duetto. Zum Abendmahls Lml.

SS;2Fl;Str;Organo(fig. bass).-G min.-*Adagio.*-83m.-Hymn 63
[Kl. Br. Ges. III].
For another version, see Herbst 236.4.

237 FREYDT, JOHANN LUDWIG (1748-1807)
[O möcht sich mit lebendgen Farben]
Aria

S;Bn;Str.-C min.-*Langsam.*-55m.-Hymn 165,8 (C. R. von Zinzendorf).
Concludes with final lines of Tune 184A.
For another version, see Herbst 237b.

237b FREYDT, JOHANN LUDWIG (1748-1807)
[O möcht sich mit lebendgen Farben]
Aria

S;Bn;Str;Fondamento(fig.bass).-C min.-*Adagio. con Sordini.*-62m.-
Hymn 165,8 (C. R. von Zinzendorf).
Concludes with final lines of Tune 184A.
For another version, see Herbst 237.

238 FREYDT, JOHANN LUDWIG (1748-1807)
[Der Friede Gottes]

SSAB;Str.-E min.-*Grave.*-64m.-Colosser 3:15.
See also Herbst 293.

239a FREYDT, JOHANN LUDWIG (1748-1807)
[Den aller Welt]

T;2Bns;Str.-B-Flat maj.-*Moderato.*-54m.-Hymn 56,3 (Luther).

239b FREYDT, JOHANN LUDWIG (1748-1807)
[Schön bist du]

SS;Str;Harpa.-C maj.-*Andante.*-99m.-Hymn.

Ad239b FREYDT, JOHANN LUDWIG (1748-1807)
[Schön bist du]

SS;Str.-B-Flat maj.-*Andante.*-89m.-Hymn.
"etwas verändert di Herbst."

240 FREYDT, JOHANN LUDWIG (1748-1807)
[Eins bitte ich]
Aria

S;Bn;Str.-A min.-50m.-Hymn 443,1 (Cammerhof).

241 FREYDT, JOHANN LUDWIG (1748-1807) *1781*
[Ihre Seele gefiel Gott]
Aria

S;Str.-E-Flat maj.-*Sehr langsam. semper piano.*-99m.-Hymn.

242   FREYDT, JOHANN LUDWIG (1748-1807) *Zum 9. Januar. 1780*
       [Ihr seyd theuer erkauft]

SSAB;Str.-C min.-*Allegro.*-51m.-I.Corinther 6:20.

243   FREYDT, JOHANN LUDWIG (1748-1807) *Zum grossen Sabbath 1780*

243.1   [Es kam, dass Er mit]
         Aria

T;Str.-F min.-38m.-Lucä 22:44.

243.2   [Der Herr gibt Gnade]
         Arietta

S;Str.-C maj.-*Vivace.*-52m.-Psalm 84:12.

244a   HERBST, JOHANNES (1735-1812) *Zum 4. May 1780*
        [Dem aber, der euch]

SSAB.-B-Flat maj.-19m.-Judä 24,25.

244b   GEISLER, JOHANN CHRISTIAN (1729-1815) *Zum 4. May 1780*
        [Dem aber, der euch]

SSAB;Str.-G-C maj.-*Gemässigt.*-82m.-Judä 24,25.

245   FREYDT, JOHANN LUDWIG (1748-1807) *Zum 8. Aug. 1780*
[Man verkündige bey den Nachkommen]

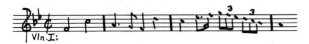

SSAB;Str.-F maj.-*Allegro non troppo.*-110m.-Psalm 48:14,15.
Losung for August 8, 1780.

246a   FREYDT, JOHANN LUDWIG (1748-1807) *Zum 8. Aug. 1780*
[Dein sind wir]

SSAB;Str.-F maj.-*Lento.*-36m.

246b   FREYDT, JOHANN LUDWIG (1748-1807) *Zum 7. Sept. 1780*

246b[.1] [Der Herr segne euch]

A/SSAB;Str.-C min.-*Grave.*-70m.-Psalm 115:14; Hymn.
Losung for September 7, 1780.
Marked No. "*2*" on ms.

246b[.2] [Fahre fort]

SSAB;flg.bass.-D maj.-*Mittelmässig langsam.* 30m.
Marked No. "*3*" on ms.

247   HERBST, JOHANNES (1735-1812) *Zum 17. Aug. 1780*

247.1   [Das ist das Geschlecht]

SSAB[or SATB] Str.-B-Flat maj.-*Moderato.*-57m.-Psalm 24:6.
SATB arr. added in red ink.
Losung for August 17, 1780.

247.2   [Heiliget Gott den Herrn]

SSAB[or SATB] ;Str.-E-Flat maj.-*Larghetto.*-47m.-I.Petri 3:15.
SATB arr. added in red ink.

248   FREYDT, JOHANN LUDWIG (1748-1807) *Zum 31. Aug. 1780*

248.1   [Ich will euch tragen]

SSAB;fig.bass.-D maj.-*Langsam.*-26m.-Jesaia 46:4

248.2   [Wer an Ihn glaubet]

SSAB;fig.bass.-C maj.-*Etwas Munter.*-20m.-Römer 9:33.
Losung for August 31, 1780.

249   GRAUN, KARL HEINRICH (1701-1759) *Zum 31. Aug. 1780*

249.1   [Ich will euch tragen]

SS;Str.-E maj.-*Andante.*-72m.-Jesaia 46:4.
Adapted from his opera, *Brittanico.* [See B IV, vol. 2, no. 23]

249.2   [Wer an Ihn glaubet]

SS;Str.-E maj.-*Adagio.*-57m.-Römer 9:33.
Losung for August 31, 1780.
Adapted from his opera, *Lucio Papirio.* [See B IV, vol. 1, no. 6]

250   HERBST, JOHANNES (1735-1812) *Zum 7. Sept. 1780*
       [Der Herr segne euch]

SSTB;Str.-E-Flat maj.-*Langsam.*-81m.-Psalm 115:14.
Losung for September 7, 1780.
Derived from Gregor's setting of the *Kirchen-Segen* [Herbst 6a, 6b].

251   FREYDT, JOHANN LUDWIG (1748-1807) *Zum 27. Oct. 1780*
       [Wohl dem, der den Herrn—Wir wollen nichts]

SSAB;Str.-B-Flat maj.-*Moderato;Choralmässig.*-44m.-Psalm 112:1;
Hymn.
Losung and Hymn for October 27, 1780.

252   HERBST, JOHANNES (1735-1812) *Zum 13. Nov 1780*
       [Wir haben ein Fest des Herrn]

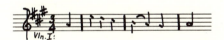

SSAB;Str/SSAB;Str.-A maj.-*Lebhaft.*-81m.-II.Mose 10:9; Lucä 1:47.
"*Nota! Das Preludium wird von beyden Chören gespielt.*"

253   HERBST, JOHANNES (1735-1812) *Zu Br. Layriz Geburtstage am 13.
       Nov. 1780*
       [Dein Alter sey wie deine Jugend]

SS;Str.-G maj.-*Lieblich.*-64m.-V.Mose 33:25.

254   FREYDT, JOHANN LUDWIG (1748-1807) *m. Decembr. 1780*
       [Siehe! Finsterniss bedeckte das Erdreich]

SSAB;Str.-D min.-*Spiritoso.*-48m.-Jesaia 60:2.

255.1 FREYDT, JOHANN LUDWIG (1748-1807) *Zum 24. Dec. 1778*
       [Welch süsser Ton!]

SSAB;Bn;Str.-F maj.-*Etwas lebhaft.*-112m.-Hymn.
For another version, see Herbst 296.2.

255.2 HERBST, JOHANNES (1735-1812) *Zum 24. Dec. 1780*
       [Heiliger Herre Gott!—Deiner Menschheit]

SSAB;Str.-D maj.-*Moderato;Etwas Munterer.*-67m.-Hymn 585
[Litany];Hymn.

256   FREYDT, JOHANN LUDWIG (1748-1807) *Zum 7. Jan. 1781*
       [Singet dem Herrn ein neues Lied. Sein Ruhm]

SSAB;Str.-C maj.-*Allegro con Spirito.*-62m.-Jesaia 42:10; Hymn 1619,2
(Herrnschmidt).
For an alternate text, see Herbst 294.1.
Losung and Hymn for January 7, 1781.

257   HERBST, JOHANNES (1735-1812) *Zum 25. Mart. 1781*
       [Nachdem die Kinder]

SSTB;Str.-D maj.-*Bedächtig.*-99m.-Ebräer 2:14; Jesaia 25:9.
Text for March 25, 1781.

258   HERBST, JOHANNES (1735-1812) *Zum 4. May 1781*
[Gesegnet bist du]

SSTB;Str.-F maj.-*Langsam.*-64m.
Losung for May 4, 1781.

259   HERBST, JOHANNES (1735-1812) *Zum Begräbniss der Schw.*
Soph. Fr. v. Seidliz am 17. May 1781
[So ruhe nun in Jesu]

SS;Str.-A min.-*Lento. con Sordini.*-101m.-Hymn.

260   FREYDT, JOHANN LUDWIG (1748-1807) *Zum 24. Juny 1781*
[Der Herr Jesus Christus—Er segne euch]

SSAB;Str.-G maj.-*Grave;Moder.*.-68m.-II.Timotheum 4:22; Hymn 665,2
(Gregor).
Text and Hymn for June 24, 1781.

261   HERBST, JOHANNES (1735-1812) *Zum Begräbniss L. M. der sel.*
Schw. v. Stojentin am 5. Aug. 1781
[O selig bist du!]

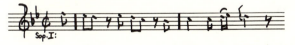

SSAB;Str.-B-Flat maj.-*Larghetto.*-35m.-Johannis 1:16.

262   FREYDT, JOHANN LUDWIG (1748-1807) *Zum 8. Aug. 1781*
        [Er ist der Heilige]

B/SSAB;Str.-D maj.-*Maestoso.*-36m.

263   FREYDT, JOHANN LUDWIG (1748-1807) *Zum 8. Aug. 1781*
        [Du solst mit einem neuen Namen]

SSAB;2Fl;2Hns;Str.-D maj.-*Nicht zu geschwind.*-44m.-Jesaia 62:2.
Losung for August 8, 1781.

264[.1] HERBST, JOHANNES (1735-1812) *Zum 29. Aug. 1781*
        [Wohl dem, dem seine Uebertretungen]

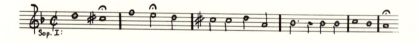

SSAB.-D min.-*Choralmässig.*-13m.-Psalm 32:1,2.

264[.2] HERBST, JOHANNES (1735-1812)
        [Nun liebes Chor]

SSAB.-D min.-18m.

264[.3] GREGOR, CHRISTIAN (1723-1801)
        [Der Herr segne dich]
        Der Kirchensegen

S;Str.-E-Flat maj.-30m.-IV.Mose 6:24-26.
See also Herbst 6b.

265   FREYDT, JOHANN LUDWIG (1748-1807) *Zum 29. Aug. 1781*
       [Wohl dem, dem seine Uebertretungen]

SSAB;Str.-B-Flat maj.-*Andante.*-86m.-Psalm 32:1,2.
2 copies.

266   HERBST, JOHANNES (1735-1812) *Zum 31. Aug. 1781*

266.1 [Sorget nicht]

SSTB;Str.-G maj.-*Andante.*-36m.-Psalm 145:18.

266.2 [Lobet den Herrn! denn Er wird]

SSTB;Str.-C maj.-*Munter.*-61m.-Psalm 89:3.
Thematic derivation from Tune 48.

266.3 [Gnade, Fried und Seligkeit]

SSTB;Str.-D maj.-*Etwas langsam.*-39m.-Hymn.

267   HERBST, JOHANNES (1735-1812) *Zum 7. Sept. 1781*
[Singet dem Herrn ein neues Lied! denn der]

SSTB;[2Cl;2Hn] ;Str.-C maj.-*Munter.*-55m.-Psalms 96:1,4; 68:5.
Cl. and Hn. pts. on separate sheet.

268   FREYDT, JOHANN LUDWIG (1748-1807) *Zum 7. Sept. 1781*
[Singet dem Herrn ein neues Lied! denn der]

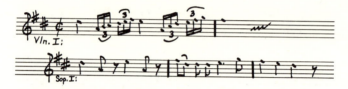

SSAB;Fl.trav;2Hn;Vln.obl;Vcl;Str;Fond.-D maj.-*Moderato.*-46m.-
Psalms 96:1; 68:5.

269   NAUMANN, JOHANN GOTTLIEB (1741-1801) *Zum 13. Nov. 1781*
[Dir o Jesu! nachzuwandeln]

SS;Str;keyboard.-G maj.-. . . *non troppo.*-61m.-Hymn.

270   NAUMANN, JOHANN GOTTLIEB (1741-1801) *Zum 13. Nov. 1781*
[Schöpfer, Erlöser, Herr Himmels]

SSTB;Str;Organo(mel, fig.bass).-C maj.-*Allegro Staccato e maestoso.*-
118m.-Hymn.
Extra vocal score on separate sheet, with incomplete soprano recitative.

271   FREYDT, JOHANN LUDWIG (1748-1807) *Zum 13. Nov. 1781*
[So lass denn deine blutge Segen]
Arietta

S;2Fl;Str.-F maj.-*Langsam.*-16m.-Hymn.

272a HERBST, JOHANNES (1735-1812) *Zum 13. Jan. 1782*
[Der Herr Zebaoth]

SSTB;Str.-D maj.-*Munter.*-32m.-Jesaia 24:23.
Losung for January 13, 1782.

272b FREYDT, JOHANN LUDWIG (1748-1807) *Zum 13. Jan. 1782*
[Der Herr Zebaoth—Du unser Friedens-König]

S/SSAB;2Fl;2Hn;Vcl.obl;Str;Organo (bass).-D maj.-*Allegr mod.;
Andante.*-91m.-Jesaia 24:23; Hymn; Tune 79A.
Losung and Hymn for January 13, 1782.

273 HERBST, JOHANNES (1735-1812) *Zum 25. Mart. 1782*

273.1 [Gott kommt und wird euch]

SSAB;Str.-A maj.-*Andante.*-47m.-Jesaia 35:4.
Losung for March 25, 1782.

273.2   [Er wird dir gnädig]

SSAB;Str.-E min.-*Langsam.*-62m.-Jesaia 30:19; Hymn.

273.3   [Der in euch angefangen]

SSAB;Str.-C maj.-*Lebhaft.*-56m.-Philipper 1:6.

274   HERBST, JOHANNES (1735-1812) *Zum grossen Sabbath 1782*
[Gott war in Christo]

SSTB;Str.;fig.bass.-D maj.-*Largo.*-72m.-II.Corinther 5:19; Hymn 134,1
(Rist).
Contains concluding lines of Tune 168A.

275.1   HOMILIUS, GOTTFRIED AUGUST (1714-1785)
[Seh ich in deinen Seelen-Schmerzen]

S/SATB;Str.-C min.-*Andante.*-118m.-Hymn.
From his *Passions-Cantate.* [See B XXII]

275.2   ROLLE, JOHANN HEINRICH (1718-1785)
[Heilge Ruhe]

SATB;Str.-E-Flat maj.-*Moderato.*-75m.-Hymn.
From his oratorio, *Lazarus: "Heilge Stätte"* [See B XXXIV]
Alternate text: *Schöner Morgen.*

276   KOZELUCH, LEOPOLD ANTON (1752-1818) *Zum Begräbniss des selig. Br. v. Wiedebach am 17. May 1782 in Niesky*
[So schlafe sanft]

SATB;Str.-G min.-*Largo. semper piano.*-84m.

277a   HERBST, JOHANNES (1735-1812) *Zum 17. Aug. 1782*
[O Jesu! der du uns versühntest]

SSTB;Str.-G maj.-*Etwas Langsam.*-44m.-Hymn.

277b   ROLLE, JOHANN HEINRICH (1718-1785)
[O Jesu! der du uns versühntest]

SSTB;Str.-B min.-*Langsam.*-51m.-Hymn.

278   HERBST, JOHANNES (1735-1812) *Zum 31. Aug. 1782*
[Ihr werdet mit Freuden]

SSTB;Str.-C maj.-*Munter.*-51m.-Jesaia 12:3.
Losung for August 31, 1782.

279   HERBST, JOHANNES (1735-1812) *Zum 7. Sept. 1782*

279.1   [Hebet eure Hände]

SSAB;Str.-F maj.-*Etwas langsam.*-12m.-Psalm 134:2.

279.2   [Der Herr will einen ewigen Bund]

SSAB;Str.-D maj.-*Munter.*-14m.-Jesaia 55:3.
Losung for September 7, 1782.

279.3   [Amen! der Herr thue also]

SSAB;Str.-C maj.-*Andante.*-17m.-Jeremia 28:6; I.Timotheum 1:17.

280   GREGOR, CHRISTIAN (1723-1801) *Zum 7. Septembr. 1782*

280.1   [Dis ist der neue Bund—Er will euer Gott seyn—Und alle eure Kinder—
           Und grosser Friede]

SSTB;Str.-B-Flat maj.-*Nicht geschwinde. Moderato; Etwas Munterer;*
Etwas langsamer.-84m.-Jeremia 31:31,33; Jesaia 54:13.
For another version, see Herbst 16.3,4,7,8.

280.2   [Amen! der Herr thue also]

SSTB;Str.-E-Flat maj.-*Andante.*-26m.-Jeremia 28:6; I.Timotheum 1:17.

281   HERBST, JOHANNES (1735-1812) *Zum 25. Mart. 1783*
[Also hat Gott die Welt]

SSAB;Str.-C maj.-*Munter, nicht zu geschwind.*-65m.-Johannis 3:16.
Text for March 25, 1783.

282   HERBST, JOHANNES (1735-1812) *Zum 4. May 1783*

282.1   [Suche heim den Weinstock]

SSAB;Str.-A maj.-*Mit Affect.*-78m.-Psalm 80:15,16; Hymn.

282.2   [Ihr habt mich nicht erwehlet]

S;Str.-D maj.-*Langsam.*-83m.-Johannis 15:16.
Text for May 4, 1783.

282.3   GAMBOLD, JOHN (1760-1795)
[Die mit Thränen säen]

S/SSAB;Str;Organo(fig.bass).-C min.-*Larghetto.*-
64m.-Psalm 126:5,6.

282.1b   GEISLER, JOHANN CHRISTIAN (1729-1815) *Zum 4. May 1783*
[Suche heim den Weinstock]

SSAB;2Fl;Str.-A maj.-*Moderato.*-109m.-Psalm 80:15,16; Hymn.

283   HASSE, JOHANN ADOLPH (1699-1783) *Zum 29. Aug. 1783*
[Wie theuer ist deine Güte]

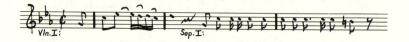

SSAB;Str.-C min.-*Larghetto.*-35m.-Psalm 36:8-10.
Adapted from Hasse's *Giuseppe Liberato:* "Defende populum
tuum." [See B XI]
See also Herbst 165.2.

284   HERBST, JOHANNES (1735-1812) *Zum 31. Aug. 1783*
[Der Herr hat Zion erwehlet]

SSTB;Str.-C maj.-*Moderato.*-66m.-Psalm 132:13,14.
Losung for August 31, 1783.

285   HERBST, JOHANNES (1735-1812) *Zum 13. Nov. 1783*

285.1   [Saget unter den Heiden]

SSTB;Str.-B-Flat maj.-*Munter doch nicht zu geschwind.*-87m.-
Psalm 96:10.
Losung for November 13, 1783.

285.2   [Einer ist euer Meister]

S;Str.-E-Flat maj.-*Langsam.*-52m.-Matthäi 23:8.
Text for November 13, 1783.
See Herbst 132.2.

286   HERBST, JOHANNES (1735-1812) *Zum 11. Jan. 1784*

286a   [Er hat uns ein Vorbild]

SSTB;Str.-D maj.-*Bedachtsam.*-62m.-I.Petri 2:21.

286b   [Er ist Jesus]

S/SSTB;Str.-D maj.-*Etwas Munter.*-40m.-I.Mose 45:4, 5.
Arranged from Christian Gregor's *Er ist Joseph* [Herbst 41].

287.1   NAUMANN, JOHANN GOTTLIEB (1741-1801) *Psalm 95 v. 1, 6, 7
zur Ehre und Lobe Gottes der Christlichen Gemeine zu Herrnhuth
zugeeignet und gewidmet*
[Kommt herzu, lasset uns—Kommt, lasset uns anbeten—Denn Er ist
unser Gott]

SSTB/SS/SSTB;Str;Cembalo.-G maj;C maj;G maj.-*Andante;Adagio;
Allegretto.*-65m;19m;75m.-Psalm 95:1,6,7.

287.2   ROLLE, JOHANN HEINRICH (1718-1785)
        [Ihr Blümlein auf der grünen Aue]

SSTB;Str.-E-Flat maj.-*Affettuoso.*-65m.-Hymn.
Alternate texts: *Nun der durchgrabnen Hände; For all the Wonders of His favour.*
For another text, see Herbst 287.3.
See also Herbst 322.1b.

287.3   ROLLE, JOHANN HEINRICH (1718-1785)
        [Ach wiederholt mir Jesu]

SSTB;Str.-E-Flat maj.-*Affettuoso.*-65m.-Hymn 164 (Louise v. Hayn).
For an alternate text, see Herbst 287.2.
See also Herbst 322.1b.

288.1   TÜRK, DANIEL GOTTLOB (1756-1813)
        [Ehre sey Gott in der Höhe]

SSTB/SSTB;Str.-D maj.-*Allegro.*-107m.-Lucä 2:14.
From his *Die Hirten bey der Krippe zu Bethlehem.* [See B XL]
For another version, see Herbst 355.

288.2   HOMILIUS, GOTTFRIED AUGUST (1714-1785)
        [Siehe, das ist Gottes Lamm]

SSTB;Str.-E-Flat maj.-*Langsam u. angenehm.*-82m.-Johannis 1:29.
From his *Passions-Cantate.* [See B XXII]

289   HERBST, JOHANNES (1735-1812) *Zum 25. Mart. 1784*
[Der Herr dein Gott wird sich]

SSTB;Str.-C maj.-*Munter.*-65m.-Zephanja 3:17.

290.1   HANDEL, GEORGE FREDERICK (1685-1759) *Zum gr. Sabbath 1768*
[Er war verachtet]

S;Str;fig.bass.-C maj.-*Largo.*-67m.
Derived from Handel's *The Messiah:* "He was despised."
See Herbst 104.6.

290.2   HERBST, JOHANNES (1735-1812)
[Fürwahr, Er trug unsre Krankheit]

SSTB;Str.-D maj.-*Langsam.*-56m.-Jesaia 53:4,5.
See Herbst 172 and 393.

291   HERBST, JOHANNES (1735-1812) *Zum 4. May 1784*
[Setzet eure Hoffnung]

SSTB;Str.-C maj.-*Etwas munter.*-55m.-I.Petri 1:13.

291b   FREYDT, JOHANN LUDWIG (1748-1807) *Aria zum 4. May 1784*
[Setzet eure Hoffnung]

S;Vln[or Fl] obl;Str;Organo (fig.bass).-F maj.-*Adagio.*-37m.-
I.Petri 1:13.

292   [UNIDENTIFIED] *Zum 15. Jul. 1784*
        [Hofft auf den Herrn]

SSB;Str;fig.bass-E-Flat maj.-*Andantino.*-110m.-Hymn.
Alternate text: Trust in the Lord.

293   FREYDT, JOHANN LUDWIG (1748-1807) *Zum 31. Aug. 1784*

293.1   [Der Friede Gottes]

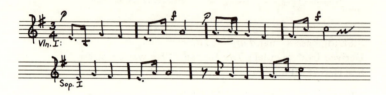

SSTB;Str.-E min.-*Grave.*-58m.-Colosser 3:15.
See also Herbst 238, 293b, 293.2: *Der Herr des Friedens.*

293.2   [Der Herr des Friedens]

SSTB[Str?].-E min.-*Grave.*-58m.-II.Thessalonicher 3:16.
Vocal score; identical with vocal pts. for Herbst 293.1 *(Der
Friede Gottes).*
Losung for August 31, 1784.

293b   FREYDT, JOHANN LUDWIG (1748-1807) *Zum 31. Aug. 1784*
        [Der Friede Gottes]

SSAB;Str;Organo(fig.bass).-E min.-*Lento.*-38m.-Colosser 3:15.
See also Herbst 238, 293.1, 293.2.

294.1   FREYDT, JOHANN LUDWIG (1748-1807) *Zum 7. Sept. 1784*
        [Singet dem Herrn ein neues Lied. Die Gemeine]

SSAB;Str.-C maj.-*Allegro con Spirito.*-60m.-Psalm 149:1.
For an alternate text, see Herbst 256.

294.2   HERBST, JOHANNES (1735-1812) *Zum 7. Sept. 1784*
[Wer sind wir Herr]

SSTB;Str.-G maj.-*Larghetto.*-51m.-II. Samuelis 7:18.

295   GEISLER, JOHANN CHRISTIAN (1729-1815) *Losung vom 29.
July 1778*
[Herr, du wollest dich]

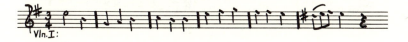

SSAB;Str.-E min.-107m.-Psalm 102:14.

296   FREYDT, JOHANN LUDWIG (1748-1807) *Zum 24. Decembr. 1778*

296.1   [Das Wort ward Fleisch]

SSAB;Str;Vcl;Organo.-E-Flat maj.-*Moderato.*-41m.-Johannis 1:14.
For another version, see Herbst 201[.3].

296.2   [Welch süsser Ton!]

SSAB;Bn;2Hn;Vcl;Organo.-F maj.-*Vivace.*-115m.-Hymn.
For another version, see Herbst 255.1.

297   GEISLER, JOHANN CHRISTIAN (1729-1815) *Zum 24. Decembr. 1779*

297.1   [Uns ist ein Kind geboren]

SSB/SSB;2Fl;Str.-G maj.-*Frölich.*-93m.-Jesaia 9:6,7.

297.2   [Freuet euch und seyd fröhlich]

SSAB;Fl;Str.-A maj.-*Mässig geschwind.*-100m.-Psalms 45:3; 104:2; 72:19.

298   GEHRA, AUGUST HEINRICH (1715-1785) *Zum 4. May 1780*

298.1   [Man singet mit Freuden]

SSAB;Str;Organo.-D maj.-*Lebhaft.*-34m.-Psalms 118:15; 89:16,17.

298.2   [Dem aber, der euch]

SSAB;Str;Organo.-D maj.-*Moderato.*-33m.-Judä 24,25.

298.3   GEBHARD, JOHANN GOTTFRIED (1755-)
[Wir wollen täglich rühmen]

SSAB;Str.-D maj.-*Lebhaft.*-81m.-Psalm 44:9.

299   GEISLER, JOHANN CHRISTIAN (1729-1815) *Zum 29. Aug. 1780*
[Unser keiner lebt ihm selber]

SSAB;2Fl;Str.-B-Flat maj.-*Lento.*-90m.-Römer 14:7,8.

300   PETER, JOHN FREDERIK (1746-1813) *Zum 7. Sept. 1780*
[Der Herr segne euch]

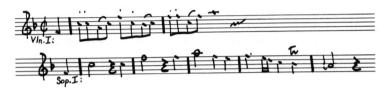

SSAB;2Fl;Str.-F maj.-*Andante con Affetto.*-40m.-Psalm 115:14.
Losung for September 7, 1780.

301.1   ROLLE, JOHANN HEINRICH (1718-1785) *Zur Christnacht 1781*
[Schönstes Kind]

SSTB;2Fl;2Hn;Str;Organo.-F maj.-*Grazioso.*-88m.-Hymn.
From his *Saul* [See B XXXIII]

301.2   GEISLER, JOHANN CHRISTIAN (1729-1815)
[Singt und spielt]

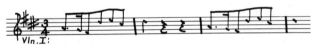

SSAB;2Fl;2Hn;Str.-D maj.-*Vivace non tanto.*-89m.-Hymn.

302.1   WOLF, ERNST WILHELM (1735-1792)
[Schlaf in Frieden]
Coro vom Capellmeister Wolf

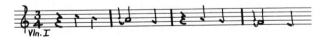

SATB;Ob;2Bn;Str;fig.bass.-C maj.-*Largo.*-118m.-Hymn.
Alternate texts: Saints and Angels join'd in concert;
Wie so selig.

302.2   GEISLER, JOHANN CHRISTIAN (1729-1815) *Zum grossen Sabbath am 30. Mart. 1782*
[Für mich, o Herr]
Coro

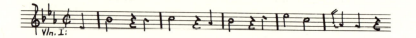

SSAB;Str.-E-Flat maj.-85m.-Hymn.

303.1   LATROBE, CHRISTIAN IGNATIUS (1758-1836) *Zum 7. Sept. 1782 in Nisky*
[Amen! der Herr thue also]

S/SATB;2 Ob;2Hn;3Trb;Vln.obl;Str;Organo (fig.bass).-E-Flat maj.-*Andante molto.*-111m.-Jeremia 28:6; I.Timotheum 1:17.

303.2   LATROBE, CHRISTIAN IGNATIUS (1758-1836) *Zum 7. Sept. 1783*
[Gleichwie ein milder Regen]
Arietta

S;Str;Organo(fig.bass).-F maj.-*Moderato.*-30m.-Hymn.

304   GEISLER, JOHANN CHRISTIAN (1729-1815) *Zum 4. May 1783*
[Die mit Thränen säen]

SSAB;2Fl;Str.-A min-C maj.-*Larghetto.*-65m.-Psalm 126:5,6.

305   FREYDT, JOHANN LUDWIG (1748-1807) *Zum 29. Aug. 1783*
[Sie werden trunken]

SSAB;2Hn;Str;Organo(fig.bass).-A maj.-*Moderato.*-64m.-Psalm 36:9.
Losung for August 29, 1783.

306   GEISLER, JOHANN CHRISTIAN (1729-1815) *Zum 31. Aug. 1783*

306.1   [Wir segnen euch]

SSAB;Str.-G maj.-*Langsam.*-40m.-Psalm 118:26.

306.2   [Wo euer Schatz ist]

SSAB;Str.-D maj.-*Lieblich.*-58m.-Matthäi 6:21.
Text for August 31, 1783.

306.3   [Der Herr hat Zion erwehlet]

SSAB;Str.-G maj.-50m.-Psalm 132:13,14.
Losung for August 31, 1783.

307   GAMBOLD, JOHN (1760-1795) *Zum 31. Aug. 1783*
       [Der Herr hat Zion erwehlet]
       Aria

T;Str;Organo(fig.bass).-C maj.-*Andante.*-62m.-Psalm 132:13,14.
Losung for August 31, 1783.

308   FREYDT, JOHANN LUDWIG (1748-1807) *Zum 13. Nov. 1783*
[Saget unter den Heiden]

SSAB;2Hn;Str;Organo(bass).-G maj.-*Maestoso.*-78m.-Psalm 96:10.
Losung for November 13, 1783.

309   FREYDT, JOHANN LUDWIG (1748-1807) *Zum 24. Dec. 1783*
[Der Herr lässet sein Heil]

SSAB;2Hn;Str;Organo(bass).-D maj.-*Allegro Moderato.*-99m.-
Psalm 98:2; Hymn.
Losung for December 24, 1783.

310   FREYDT, JOHANN LUDWIG (1748-1807) *Zum 11. Jan. 1784*
[Es wird sehr lichte—Die wahre Gnadensonne]

SSAB;2Hn;Vln.obl;Str;Organo(bass).-D maj.-*Maestoso. Allegro mod;
Grazioso.*-101m.-Ezechiel 43:2; Hymn 87,1 (Zinzendorf).
Losung and Hymn for January 11, 1784.

311   FREYDT, JOHANN LUDWIG (1748-1807) *Zum 7. Sept. 1784*
[Singet dem Herrn ein neues Lied. Die Gemeine]

SSAB/SSAB;2Hn;Str;Organo(fig.bass).-C maj.-*Vivace.*-38m.-
Psalm 149:1.

312   FREYDT, JOHANN LUDWIG (1748-1807) *Zum 25. Martius 1785*
[Lobet den Herrn, denn Er ist]

SSAB;[2Fl;2Cl;2Hn] ;Str;2Harpa;Cembalo;Fundam.(fig.bass).-C maj.-
Vivace.-100m.-Psalm 135:3.
Flute, clarinet, and horn pts. on separate sheet.

313   HERBST, JOHANNES (1735-1812) *Zum 4. May 1785*

313.1 [Die Liebe Gottes]

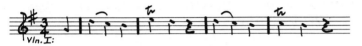

SSTB;Str.-G maj.-*Lieblich.*-101m.-Römer 5:5
Text for May 4, 1785.

313.2 [Suchet sein Antlitz]

SSTB;Str.-C maj.-*Bedachtsam.*-74m.-Psalms 105:4; 34:6.
Losung for May 4, 1785.

314   FREYDT, JOHANN LUDWIG (1748-1807) *Zum 17. Aug. 1785*
       [Wir wollen täglich rühmen]

SSAB;2Hn;Str.-G maj.-*Andantino.*-67m.-Psalm 44:9.
Losung for August 17, 1785.

315.1 FREYDT, JOHANN LUDWIG (1748-1807) *Zum 29. Aug. 1785*
       [Die Gnade und Wahrheit]

SSAB;2Hn;Str;Organo(fig.bass).-B-Flat maj.-*Allegro moderato.*-
61m.-Psalm 117:2.
Losung for August 29, 1785.

315.2 HERBST, JOHANNES (1735-1812) *Zum 29. Aug. 1785*
[Sie werden trunken]

SSTB;Str.-C maj.-*Munter.*-57m.-Psalm 36:9.

316.1 GEISLER, JOHANN CHRISTIAN (1729-1815) *Zum 7. Sept. 1783*
[Das Blut Jesu Christi]

SSAB;Str.-G maj.-*Andante.*-76m.-I.Johannis 1:7.
A second copy: transposed to F major.

316.2 HERBST, JOHANNES (1735-1812) *Zum 7. Sept. 1785*
[Wohl denen, die den Herrn]

SSTB;[2Hn] ;Str.-C maj.-*Munter.*-61m.-Psalm 84:6; 32:8; 29:11.
Horn pts. on separate sheet.

316.3 LATROBE, CHRISTIAN IGNATIUS (1758-1836) *den 7. Sept. 1783*
[Nun liebes Chor]

SSAB;Str;Organ(fig.bass).-F maj.-51m.-Hymn.
For another version, see Herbst 375.2.

317.1 FREYDT, JOHANN LUDWIG (1748-1807) *Zum 7. Sept. 1782*
[Hebet eure Hände]

SSAB;[2Cl;2Bn];2Hn;Str;Organo(bass).-F maj.-*Largo;Vivace.*-96m.-
Psalm 134.2.
Score for Cl. and Bn. on separate sheet.

317.2   FREYDT, JOHANN LUDWIG (1748-1807)
        [Alles was Othem hat—Ach wär ein jeder Puls]

S/SSAB;[2Fl;2Cl;Bn];Bn.obl;2Hn;Str;Organ obl.-F maj.-*Vivace;
Adagio.*-148m.-Psalm 150:6; Hymn 1376,2 (Zinzendorf).
Score for flutes, clarinets and bassoon on separate sheet.
See also Herbst 233.2.

318.1   MALDERE, PIERRE VAN (1724-1768)
        [Ach wiederholt mir Jesu]
        Coro. unter ein Mittelstück einer Symphonie von Maldere

SS;2Fl;Str.-A-Flat maj.-*Grave.*-81m.-Hymn 164 (Louise v. Hayn).

318.2   ROLLE, JOHANN HEINRICH (1718-1785)
        [Ruhe sanft]
        Partitur von Rollens Composition.

SATB;Str.-C maj.-*Andante piu tosto allegretto.*-72m.-Hymn.
Adapted from Rolle's *Lazarus:* "Wiedersehn sey uns gesegnet."
[See B XXXIII]

319   FREYDT, JOHANN LUDWIG (1748-1807)
[Ach wiederholt mir Jesu]
Aria

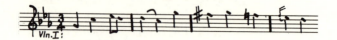

S;Str;Organo(fig.bass).-C min.-*Largo con Affettuoso. con Sordini.*-
60m.-Hymn 164.

320   LATROBE, CHRISTIAN IGNATIUS (1758-1836)
[Ruhe sanft]

TB/SATB;Fl.solo;2Cl;Str;Organo(fig.bass).-A maj.-*Poco Lento.*-
128m.-Hymn.

321   LATROBE, CHRISTIAN IGNATIUS (1758-1836) *den 8. Aug. 1783*
in Nisky
[Denn dein ist das Reich]

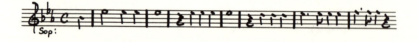

SSSATB;2Ob;2Hn;Str;Organo(fig.bass).-E-Flat maj.-*Andante.*-72m.-
Matthäi 6:13; Hymn.
Text for August 8, 1783.

322.1   FREYDT, JOHANN LUDWIG (1748-1807) *Zum grossen Sabbath 1783*
[Seh ich in deinen Seelen-Schmerzen]

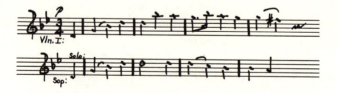

S/SSAB;2Bn;Str;Organo(bass).-G min.-*Poco Largo. Affettuoso.*-97m.-
Hymn.

322.1b ROLLE, JOHANN HEINRICH (1718-1785)
[Seh ich in deinen Seelen-Schmerzen]

SATB;2 Ob;2Hn;Str;Fondam.-E-Flat maj.-*Affettuoso.*-59m.-Hymn.
See Herbst 287.2, 287.3.

322.2 LATROBE, CHRISTIAN IGNATIUS (1758-1836)
[Heilge Ruhe]

T/SATB/SATB;2Hn;Vln.obl;Str;Organo(fig.bass).-C min.-*Andante.*-
139m.-Hymn.
A second copy: arranged for SATB/SSAB;2Hn;Str.

323.1 WEBER, GOTTFRIED (1779-1839)
[Lasset uns aufsehen]

SSAB;Str.-D maj.-64m.-Ebräer 12:2.

323.2 WEBER, GOTTFRIED (1779-1839)
[Das Lamm kam]

SSAB;Str.-E-Flat maj;B-Flat maj.-53m.-Offenbarung 5:7; Hymn 368,9.

324a.1 LATROBE, CHRISTIAN IGNATIUS (1758-1836)
[Ehre sey dem]

B/SSAB;2 Ob;2Trpt.or Hn;Trb;Str(2Vln,2Vla,Vcl,Violono);Organo
(fig.bass).-D maj.-*Andante maestoso.*-106m.-Johannis 11:25,26.
For another version, see Herbst 324b.

324a.2 LATROBE, CHRISTIAN IGNATIUS (1758-1836)
[Einer ist euer Meister]

S/SATB;Str;Organo(fig.bass).-D maj.-*Andante.*-53m.-
Matthäi 23:8.

324b LATROBE, CHRISTIAN IGNATIUS (1758-1836)
[Ehre sey dem]

B/SSAB;2Trpt or Hns;Str;Fondamento.-D maj.-*Andante maestoso.*-
92m.-Johannis 11:25,26.
For another version, see Herbst 324a.1.

325 LATROBE, CHRISTIAN IGNATIUS (1758-1836)
[Nun erschallt vor Deinem Throne]

T/SATB/SATB;2Hn;2Trpt;Str;Organo(fig.bass).-C maj.-*Andante.*-
208m.-Hymn.

326   GEISLER, JOHANN CHRISTIAN (1729-1815)
[Du bist gesegnet]

SSTB;Str.-D maj.-*Fröhlich doch nicht zu geschwind.*-44m.-I.Mose 27:33.

327   GEHRA, AUGUST HEINRICH (1715-1785)
[Das Loos ist mir gefallen]

SSAB;Str;Cembalo.-F maj.-*Moderato.*-90m.-Psalm 16:6.

328.1   VERBEEK, JOHANN RENATUS (1748-1820)
[Die Liebe Gottes]

S/SSAB;Str.-A maj.-*Moderato.*-75m.-Römer 5:5.

328.2   VERBEEK, JOHANN RENATUS (1748-1820)
[Freuet euch Gottes eures Heilands]

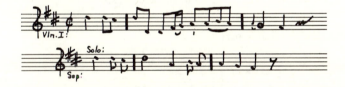

S/SSAB;Str.-D maj.-*Allegretto.*-64m.

329   FREYDT, JOHANN LUDWIG (1748-1807) *Zum 7. Sept. 1785*
[Er hat Seinen Namen]

SSAB;2Hn;Str;Organo(fig.bass).-C maj.-*Moderato.*-50m.-Psalm 138:2.
Losung for September 7, 1785.

330   HERBST, JOHANNES (1735-1812) *Zum 13. Jan. 1786*
        [Ehre sey unserm Heiland!]

SSTB;Str.-E-Flat maj.-*Grave.*-35m.

331   PETER, JOHN FREDERIK (1746-1813) *Losung zum 7. Sept. 1786*
        [Ihr sollt an Jerusalem]

SSAB;2Fl;2Hn;Str;Fond.-G maj.-*Munter u. frölich.*-69m.-
Jesaia 66:13,14.

332   PETER, JOHN FREDERIK (1746-1813) *Zum 13. Nov. 1786*

332.1   [Der Herr ist in Seinem heiligen Tempel]

S;Str.-E-Flat maj.-*Poco.* . . . .-49m.-Habacuc 2:20.
Defective ms.

332.2   [Nun bekräftige dein Wort]

SSAB;Str.-G maj.-*Lebhaft mit Nachdruck.*-27m.-Hymn.
Note at beginning: *"kan auch als ein Choral gesungen werden".*
Defective ms.

333   HERBST, JOHANNES (1735-1812) *Zur Einweyhung des neuen
        Kirchensaals in Lititz am 13. Aug. 1787*
        [Lobet den Herrn alle Seine Heerschaaren]

SATB/SSAB;2Hn;Str.-B-flat maj.-*Munter.*-55m.-Psalm 103:21.
Losung for August 13, 1787.

334   PETER, JOHN FREDERIK (1746-1813) *Losung zum 13. Nov. 1787*
[Es segne uns Gott]

SSAB;Str.-E-flat maj.-*Poco Adagio.*-26m.-Psalm 67:7.

335   PETER, JOHN FREDERIK (1746-1813) *Losung zum 14. Nov. 1787*
[Ihre Priester will ich]

SSAB;2Fl;2Trpt;Str;Fond.-B-Flat maj.-*Vivace.*-61m.-Psalm 132:16.

336   PETER, JOHN FREDERIK (1746-1813) *Losung zum 25. Dec. 1787*
[Deine Priester lass sich kleiden]

SSTB/SSAB;2Fl;2Ob;2Trpt;2Hn,Str,Fondo.-D maj.-*Vivace.* 74m.-
Psalm 132:9.
Note at beginning: "*So vollstimmig, als möglich, mit Sängern zu
besetzen*".

337   PETER, JOHN FREDERIK (1746-1813) *Zum 4. May 1788*
[Die mit Thränen säen]

SSAB;Fl;Str.-A min.-*Andante.*-68m.-Psalm 126:5,6.

338 PETER, JOHN FREDERIK (1746-1813) *Zum 29. Aug. 1788*
[Amen, der Herr thue also]

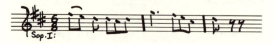

SSAB;2Trpt;Str;Fond.-D maj.-*Allegretto.*-24m.-Jeremia 28:6;
I.Timotheum 1:17.

339 PETER, JOHN FREDERIK (1746-1813) *Zur Einweyhung des
Kirchensaals in Bethabara d. 26. Nov. 1788*
[So spricht der Herr Zebaoth: Es soll]

SSB;2Fl;2Hn;Str.-E-Flat maj.-*Poco Vivace.*-56m.-Sacharja 1:17.
Losung for November 26, 1788.

340a HERBST, JOHANNES (1735-1812) *Zum 24. Dec. 1789*
[Hier schläft es]

B;Str.-D maj.-*Andante.*-83m.
For another version, see Herbst 340b.
Text on ms: *Da schläft es.*

340b HERBST, JOHANNES (1735-1812) *Zum 24. Dec. 1789*
[Hier schläft es]

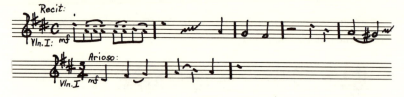

SB/SSAB;2Fl;2Hn;Str.-D maj.-*Andante;Andantino.*-83m.
For another version, see Herbst 340a.

341.1 VERBEEK, JOHANN RENATUS (1748-1820)
[Suchet sein Antlitz]

S/SSAB;Str.-D maj.-*Andante.*-69m.-Psalms 105:4; 34:6.

341.2 ?GREGOR, CHRISTIAN (1723-1801)
[Unser keiner lebt ihm selber]

SS;Str.-G maj.-*Andante.*-91m.-Römer 14:7,8.

342 HERBST, JOHANNES (1735-1812) *Zum gr. Sabbath 1790*
[Sie flochten Ihm eine Dornenkrone]

SSAB;Str.-E-Flat maj.-*Langsam.*-70m.-Matthäi 27:29.
2 copies.

343 GEISLER, JOHANN CHRISTIAN (1729-1815) *Zum 7. Sept. 1786*
[Wer dem Herrn anhanget]

SSTB;Str.-A maj.-*Andante.*-44m.-I.Corinther 6:17; Hymn.
Vocal score for SSAB on separate sheet.

344a GEISLER, JOHANN CHRISTIAN (1729-1815) *Zum Abend des
Charfreitags. d. 6. Apr. 1787*
[Das Passionsgetöne]

ST;Str/SS;Str;Orgel(bass).-E-Flat maj.-*Angenehm u. langsam.*-93m.-
Hymn 147,13 (C. R. von Zinzendorf).

344b   GEISLER, JOHANN CHRISTIAN (1729-1815)
      [Das Passionsgetöne]

SS/SS;Str.-E-Flat maj.-*Angenehm u. langsam.*-93m.-Hymn 147,13
(C.R. von Zinzendorf).

345   GEISLER, JOHANN CHRISTIAN (1729-1815) *Zum 31. Aug. 1787*

345.1   [Sehet welch eine Liebe]
      Duetto

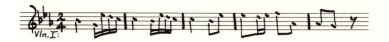

SS;Str.-E-Flat maj.-*Molto andante.*-57m.-I.Johannis 3:1.
Text for August 31, 1787.

345.2   [Du hast uns erlöset]

SSAB;[Str].-B-Flat maj.-34m.-Psalm 31:6; Klaglieder 3:22,23;
Jesaia 38:17; Ezechiel 36:11; Psalms 65:12; 111:9.
Instruments double vocal pts.

346   GEISLER, CHRISTIAN GOTTFRIED (1730-1810)
      [O wie will ich noch reden]

SSAB;2Fl;Str;Fondamento(fig.bass).-G maj.-*Lebhaft.*-79m.

347   HANDEL, GEORGE FREDERICK (1685-1759)
      [Würdig ist das Lamm]

SATB;Str.-D maj.-*Largo.*-31m.-Offenbarung 5:12.

348   GRIMM, JOHANN DANIEL (1719-1760)
[Heilge Marterstätte]
Aria

S;Str.-D min.-*Largo.*-46m.-Hymn.

349   GEISLER, JOHANN CHRISTIAN (1729-1815) *Zu Weynachten*

349.1   [Ach dass die Hülfe]

SSTB;Str.-D maj.-*Langsam.*-57m.-Psalm 14:7.

349.2   [O du zu meinem Trost]
Duetto.

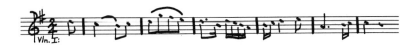

SS;Str.-G maj.-*Affettuoso.*-104m.-Hymn.

350   GEISLER, JOHANN CHRISTIAN (1729-1815) *Zu Ostern*

350.1   [Ehre sey dem]

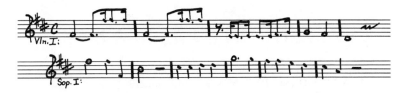

TT/SATB;2Fl;2Hn;Str;Vcl;Organo(bass).-D maj.-*Poco Allegro.*-98m.-
Johannis 11:25,26.

350.2   [Alles was Othem hat]

SATB;2Fl;2Hn;Str;Vcl;Fondamento.-D maj.-*Poco allegro.*-73m.-
Psalm 150:6.

351   HERBST, JOHANNES (1735-1812)
       [Lob und Preis und Ehre! dem unschuldigen]

SSAB;Str.-D maj.-*Munter.*-64m.

352   HERBST, JOHANNES (1735-1812) *Zum 4. May 1793*
       [Lasset uns lobsingen]

SSAB;Str.-C maj.-*Lebhaft.*-88m.-Hymn.
2 copies.

353   HERBST, JOHANNES (1735-1812) *Zum 13. Aug. 1793*
       [Gehe hin mit Frieden]

SSAB;Str.-C maj.-*Bedächtig.*-98m.-I.Samuelis 1:17.
Losung for August 13, 1793.

354a   VAN VLECK, JACOB (1751-1831) *Zu Weynachten*
       [Singt ihr Erlösten]

SSAB;Str.-D maj.-*Allegretto.*-65m.-Hymn 581,4 (Neihser).

354b HERBST, JOHANNES (1735-1812) *Zum 24. Decembr. 1793*
[Singt ihr Erlösten]

SSAB;Str.-D maj.-*Lebhaft.*-87m.-Hymn 581,4 (Neihser).
Contains written indications for 2 choirs.

355 TÜRK, DANIEL GOTTLOB (1756-1813) *Zum 24. Dec. 1793*
[Ehre sey Gott in der Höhe]

SSAB/SSAB;Str.-D maj.-*Allegro.*-85m.-Lucä 2:14.
From his *Die Hirten bey der Krippe zu Bethlehem.* [See B XL]
Marked No. "2" on title page: "1. *Hier schläft es . /Partitur s*
No. 340 [Herbst 340]/*di Herbst.*"
For another version, see Herbst 288.1.

356 REICHARDT, JOHANN FRIEDRICH (1752-1814) *Zum 4. May 1794*
[Lasset uns Ihn lieben]

SSAB;Str.-F maj.-*Allegretto.*-70m.-I.Johannis 4:19.
From his *Weihnachts-Cantilene*, no. 8. [See B XXXI]

357.1   FREYDT, JOHANN LUDWIG (1748-1807)
        [Wohl dem Volke, dess der Herr]

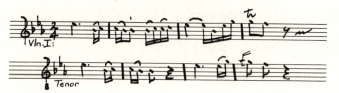

T/SATB;2Cl;2Hn;Str;Fondamento.-E-Flat maj.-*Allegro moderato.-*
88m.-Psalm 33:12.

357.2   JAESCHKE, CHRISTIAN DAVID (1755-1827)
        [Eins bitte ich]

S/SATB; Str;Vcl; Harpa; Organo.-F maj.-*Poco Andante.*-105m.-Psalm 27:4.
Harpa pt. on separate sheet.

357.3   GLUCK, CHRISTOPH WILLIBALD (1714-1787)
        [Gemein! die Freud am Herrn]
        Aria

S;Str.-E-flat maj.-*Andantino, dolce.*-74m.-Hymn.

358   GEISLER, JOHANN CHRISTIAN (1729-1815) *Zum Pfingstfest*

358.1   [Der heilige Geist]

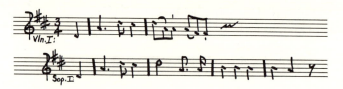

SSAB;2Hn;Str;Fondamento.-D maj.-*Lieblich u. ernsthaft.*-
63m.-Epheser 1:14.

358.2   [Die Frucht des Geistes]

SSAB;Fl;Str;Vcl;Organo(bass).-A maj.-*Angenehm u. frölich.*-
87m.-Galater 5:22.

358.3   [Der Geist, der ein Geist]

SSAB;Str;Fondamento.-E maj.-*Angenehm u. mässig langsam.*-
53m.-I.Petri 4:14.

358.4   [Er hat noch mehr]

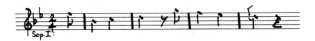

SSTB;Str.-B-Flat maj.-*Molto andante.*-50m.

359.1   GAMBOLD, JOHN (1760-1795)
         [Gott ists, der in euch wirket—Er und Seine Gnad']

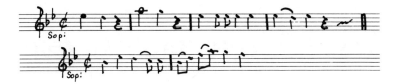

SATB;Str.-E-Flat maj.-*Grave;Andante.*-44m.-Philipper 2:13; Hymn.

359.2   MORTIMER, PETER (1750-1828)
         [Ehre sey unserm Heiland!]

SATB;Str.-D maj.-*Largo;Grave.*-43m.

359.3   FREYDT, JOHANN LUDWIG (1748-1807)
        [Der in euch angefangen]

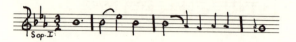

SSAB;Str.-E-Flat maj.-*Gesetzt u. nicht zu langsam.*-24m.-Philippei 1:6.

359.4   PETER, JOHN FREDERIK (1746-1813)
        [Lobe den Herrn meine Seele]

SSAB;Str.-A maj.-*Vivace.*-89m.-Psalm 103:2-4.

360   HERBST, JOHANNES (1735-1812) *Zum 4. May 1796*

360.1   [Das ist ein köstlich Ding]

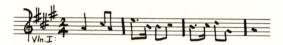

SSAB;Str.-A maj.-*Vivace.*-76m.-Psalm 92:2.
Alternate text: *Wir wollen der Güte des Herrn.*
A second, unnumbered, copy: marked by Herbst as the property of
"*Jac. van Vleck*'".

360.2   [Ich lasse dich nicht]

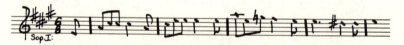

SSAB;Str.-A maj.-*Larghetto.*-58m.-Hymn.
A second, unnumbered, copy: marked by Herbst as the property of
"*Jacob van Vleck*".

360.3   [Dennoch werden wir]

SSAB;Str.-D maj.- *Andantino.*-53m.-Hymn.
A second, unnumbered, copy: marked by Herbst as the property of
"*Jacob van Vleck*".

360.4 [Der Gott des Friedens]

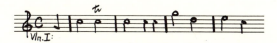

SSAB;Str.-C maj.-*Moderato.*-76m.-I.Thessalonicher 5:23,24.
A second, unnumbered, copy: marked by Herbst as the property of
"*Jacob van Vleck*".

361.1 PETER, JOHN FREDERIK (1746-1813) *Zum 17. Aug. 1774*
       [Lasset das Wort Christi]

SSAB;Str.-B-Flat maj.-*Vivace. Poco Allegro.*-102m.-Colosser 3:16.

361.2 PETER, JOHN FREDERIK (1746-1813) *Zum 31. Aug. 1775*
       [Er wird dir gnädig]

SSAB;Str.-B-Flat maj.-*Affettuoso.*-77m.-Jesaia 30:19.

361.3 PETER, JOHN FREDERIK (1746-1813)
       [Kommt lasset uns anbeten]

SSAB;Str.-F maj.-*Andante Vivace. Nachdrücklich u. etwas lebhaft.*-
61m.-Psalm 95:6.

361.4 PETER, JOHN FREDERIK (1746-1813)
       [Wohl denen, die in deinem Hause]

SSAB;Str.-D maj.-*Vivace.*-54m.-Psalm 84:5.

361.5 PETER, JOHN FREDERIK (1746-1813) *Losung zum 7. Sept. 1785*
[Du hast deinen Namen]

SSAB;Str.-E-Flat maj.-*Munter doch nicht zu geschwinde*-46m.-
Psalm 138:2.

362.1 PETER, JOHN FREDERICK (1746-1813) *Loosung zu Ostern d. 8.
Apr. 1787*
[Ich will dem Herrn singen]

SSAB;Str.-D maj.-*Vivace.*-92m.-Psalm 13:6; Hymn 203,4 (Gregor).

362.2 PETER, JOHN FREDERIK (1746-1813) *Loosung zum 24. Juny 1787*
[Herr, wie sind deine Werke]

SSAB;Str.-B-Flat maj.-*Munter.*-46m.-Psalm 92:6.

362.3 PETER, JOHN FREDERIK (1746-1813)
Loosung zum Knabenfest d. 13. Jan. 1770
[Ich will bald ihr Heiland seyn]

SSAB;Str.-G maj.-*Andante.*-61m.-Ezechiel 11:16; Hymn.

362.4 PETER, JOHN FREDERIK (1746-1813) *Loosung zum 24. Juny 1789*
[Sie sollen, spricht der Herr Zebaoth]

SSAB;Str.-F maj.-*Poco vivace.*-26m.-Maleachi 3:17.

362.5   PETER, JOHN FREDERIK (1746-1813) *Loosung zum 22. May 1793*
[Herr, deine rechte Hand—Das haben wir]

SSAB;Str.-G maj.-*Vivace;Moderato.*-58m.-II.Mose 15:6; Hymn.

363   PETER, JOHN FREDERIK (1746-1813) *Loosung zum 24. Mart. 1795*
[Nicht uns, Herr]

SSTB;2Fl;2Hn;Str;Organo.-E-Flat maj.-*Maestoso con Grave e moto.*-
72m.-Psalm 115:1.

364.1   PETER, JOHN FREDERIK (1746-1813) *Zum 29. Aug. 1786*
[In allen Dingen]

SS;Str.-B-Flat maj.-*Vivace.*-67m.-II.Corinther 6:4.

364.2   PETER, JOHN FREDERIK (1746-1813) *Los*[ung] *zum 26. Dec. 1787*
[Ich will dir ein Freudenopfer]

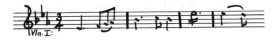

SSTB;2Hn;Str.-E-Flat maj.-*Munter.*-74m.-Psalm 54:8.

364.3   PETER, JOHN FREDERIK (1746-1813) *Losung zum gr. Sabbath d. 11. Apr. 1789*
[Der Herr ist mein Theil]

SSAB;Fl;Vcl;Str.-B-Flat maj.-*Andante vivace.*-52m.-Klaglieder 3:24.

365.1   PETER, JOHN FREDERIK (1746-1813) *Loosung zum 13. Aug. 1789*
[Er wird mich ans Licht]

SSAB;Fl;Str.-A maj.-*Munter.*-61m.-Micha 7:9.

365.2   PETER, JOHN FREDERIK (1746-1813) *Loosung zum 13. Nov. 1789*
[Da du anfingest zu beten]

S/SSAB;Fl;Str;Vcl.-G maj.-*Munter u. gesetzt.*-36m.-Daniel 9:23.

366   ANTES, JOHN (1740-1811)
[I will greatly rejoice in the Lord]

SSAB;2Hn;Str;Fond.-F maj.-*Allegro.*-155m.-Isaiah 61:10.

367   ANTES, JOHN (1740-1811)

367.1   [Go, Congregation, go]

S;Str.-C min.-*Adagio.*-43m.-Hymn 77 (Gregor) [in *Collection of Hymns,*. . .1789.]

367.2   [Surely He has borne our Grief]

SSAB;Str.-C min.-*Grave.*-34m.-Isaiah 53:4,5.

368.1   ANTES, JOHN (1740-1811)
         [Worthy is the Lamb]

SSAB;2 Ob;2Hn[or Trpt] ;Str;Fond.-D maj.-*Allegro.*-124m.-
Revelation 5:12,13.

368.2   ANTES, JOHN (1740-1811)
         [Unto us a Child is born]

SSAB;2 Ob;2Hn;Str;Fond.-D maj.-*Allegro.*-162m.-Isaiah 9:6.
"NB. It would be full as well, if the Horns & Hautbois begun only
with the forte at the 5th Bar."

368.3   ANTES, JOHN (1740-1811)
        [Lo! This is our God]

SSAB;2Hn;Str.-D maj.-*Grave;Allegro.*-88m.-Isaiah 25:9.

369   ANTES, JOHN (1740-1811)
        [Give thanks unto the Lord]

SSAB;Str.-B-Flat maj.-*Andante.*-108m.-I.Chronicles 16:34,35,10,11.

370   HERBST, JOHANNES (1735-1812) *Zum 4. May 1798*

370.1   [Ich wohne unter meinem Volk]

SSAB;Str.-F maj.-*Angenehm.*-71m.

370.2   [Also spricht der Hohe]

SSAB;Str.-C min.-*Langsam.*-63m.-Jesaia 57:15.

370.3   [Selig sind, die reines Herzens]

SSAB;Str.-B-Flat maj.-*Moderato.*-89m.-Matthäi 5:8.

371a HERBST, JOHANNES (1735-1812)
[So spricht der Herr: Siehe, ich vertilge]

SSAB;Str.-F maj.-*Lebhaft, aber nicht zu geschwind.*-32m.-
Jesaia 44:22,23.

371b PETER, JOHN FREDERIK (1746-1813)
[So spricht der Herr: Siehe, ich vertilge]
Solo con Coro

Organo pt. only.-F maj.-*Andante poco Adagio.*-82m.-Jesaia 44:22.
Ms. marked *"Litiz."*

372 HERBST, JOHANNES (1735-1812) *Zum 4. May 1800*
[Ich freue mich]

SSAB;Str.-B-Flat maj.-*Vivace.*-85m.-Jesaia 61:10.
2 copies.

373 HERBST, JOHANNES (1735-1812) *Zum 4. May 1804*

373.1 [Wir sind Glieder]

SSAB;Str.-F maj.-*Mässig.*-52m.-Epheser 5:30.

373.2   [Auf Sein vollgültigs Blut]

SSAB;Str.-A maj.-*Etwas lebhaft.*-59m.-Hymn.

373.3   HERBST, JOHANNES (1735-1812) *Zum 4. Juny 1804*
         [Schätzt recht hoch]

SSAB;Str.-G maj.-*Angenehm.*-64m.-Hymn.
Alternate text: Hark a voice devideth the Skye.

374   REICHARDT, JOHANN FRIEDRICH (1752-1814)
       [Für deine schwere Seelen-Angst]

SATB;Str.-C maj.-*Moderato assai.*-66m.
From his *Der 65te Psalm*, no. 1. [See B XXIX]

375.1   HERBST, JOHANNES (1735-1812)
         [Das Blut Jesu Christi]

SSAB;Str.-F maj.-*Andante.*-64m.-I.Johannis 1:7.

375.2   LATROBE, CHRISTIAN IGNATIUS (1758-1836)
         [Nun liebes Chor]

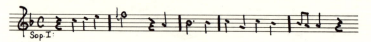

SSAB;Str.-F maj.-*Larghetto.*-41m.-Hymn.
For another version, see Herbst 316.3.

376.1   HANDEL, GEORGE FREDERICK (1685-1759)

[Siehe, das ist unser Gott]

SS/SS;Str.-E-Flat maj.-*Andante, Larghetto.*-52m.-Jesaia 25:9.
See also Herbst 461.
2 copies.

376.2   REICHARDT, JOHANN FRIEDRICH (1752-1814)
      [Ehre sey Gott in der Höhe]

SATB/SSAB;2Fl;2 Ob;2Bn;2Hn;Str;Organo(bass).-G maj.-*Maestoso.*-
76m.-Lucä 2:14.
From his *Trauer Cantata.* [See B XXX]
2 copies.

377   HANDEL, GEORGE FREDERICK (1685-1759)
      [Jesus neigte Sein Haupt—O die Minut]

SATB;Str.-F min.-*Grave.*-59m.-Johannis 19:30; Hymn 175:4,5
(C.R. von Zinzendorf); Tune 14A.
2 copies.

378   GEBHARD, JOHANN GOTTFRIED (1755-)

378.1   [Wer sind diese—Amen! Lob und Ehre]

S/SSAB solo;Organo(fig.bass);SSAB;2Hns;Trpt"*Clarino*";
4Trb(SATB);Organo(fig.bass).-B-Flat maj.-*Moderato,*
Andante affettuoso;Maestoso.-64m.-Offenbarung 7:9-15.

378.2 [Das Loos ist mir gefallen—Ich ruhe nun]

S;Str;Organo(fig.bass)/SSAB;Organo.-B-flat maj.-*Andante.-*
132m.-Psalm 16:6; Hymn 465,7 (J.F.Richter); Tune 114, var.
Psalm (solo) interspersed with lines of chorale (tutti).
Alternate text for chorale: *So ruhe sanft,* added in another hand.

378.3 [Die Gnade und Wahrheit—Drum stimmet lieblich]

SSAB;2 Ob;2Hn;Str;Fond(fig.bass)/SB;2 Ob;Str;fig.bass.-D maj;G maj;
D maj.-*Lebhaft;Langsamer;Lebhaft.*-119m.-Psalm 117:2; Hymn.

379 GEBHARD, JOHANN GOTTFRIED (1755-   )

379.1 [Preise Jerusalem den Herrn]

SSAB;2Hn;Str;Fondamento(fig.bass).-D maj.-*Maestoso.*-95m.-
Psalm 147:12-14.

379.2 [Singt dem Herrn ein neues Lied, denn der]

SATB;2Fl;2Hn;Str;Fondam.(fig.bass).-D maj.-*Munter.*-87m.-
Psalms 96:1,4; 68:5.

380 GAMBOLD, JOHN (1760-1795)

380.1   [Blutge Leiden]

SSAB;Str.-A min.-*Largo.*-54m.-Hymn 169,1 (C.L.Brau).
For another copy, see Herbst [473.1].

380.2   [Ich seh in bangen Buss-Ideen]

SSAB;Str.-D min.-*Lento e sostenuto.*-28m.-Hymn 165,1
(C.R.v.Zinzendorf).
For another copy, see Herbst [473.2].

380.3   [Todesblick, der mir mein Herz]

SSAB;Str.-G min.-*Largo espressivo.*-22m.-Hymn 169,2 (C.L.Brau).
For another copy, see Herbst [473.3].

380.4   [Deines Todes Trost]

SSAB;Str.-B-Flat maj.-*Andante.*-50m.-Hymn 139,2 (Gregor).
For another copy, see Herbst [473.4].

381   [UNIDENTIFIED]
[Sehet, welch eine Liebe]
Duetto

SS;Str.-F maj.-*Mässig.*-62m.-I.Johannis 3:1.

382   SCHULZ, JOHANN ABRAHAM PETER (1747-1800) *aus Kapellmeister Schulzens Hymns*

382.1   [Herr, unser Gott! sey hoch gepreisst!]

SATB;Str.-D maj.-*Largo maestoso.*-24m.-Hymn.

382.2   [Erhebt den Herrn]
Coro.

SATB;[2Trpt"*Clarini*"] ;Str.-D maj.-*Allegro.*-99m.
Trpt. pts. on last page.

383   GAMBOLD, JOHN (1760-1795)
[Jesus ward ein Mensch]

SS;bass.-F maj.-*Andante con moto.*-8m.-Hymn 367,1-3 (Gregor).
See also Herbst 395.2.

383.1   SCHULZ, JOHANN ABRAHAM PETER (1747-1800)
[Singet, singt mit frohem Mund]

SSTB;Str;keyboard.-E-Flat maj.-*Moderato.*-53m.
From his oratorio *Maria und Johannes*, no. 13. [See B XXXIX]

383.2   SCHULZ, JOHANN ABRAHAM PETER (1747-1800)
[O welch ein Wunder]

SSTB;Str;keyboard.-F maj.-*Andante grazioso.*-155m.
From his oratorio *Maria und Johannes,* no. 9. [See B XXXIX]

384.1   RIESS, JOHANN HEINRICH (1768-1831)
[Ich will euch tragen]

SATB;Str.-F maj.-*Poco Allegro.*-58m.-Jesaia 46:4.

384.2   RIESS, JOHANN HEINRICH (1768-1831) *Zur Christnacht 1795*
[Siehe, das ist unser Gott—Lobsingt Seinen Namen]

SATB;Str.-A maj.-*Etwas munter u. mässig.*-105m.-Jesaia 25:9.

385.1   [UNIDENTIFIED]
[Er ist der gute Hirte]

B/SSTB;Str.-D maj.-*Cantabile.*-73m.-Johannis 10:12,3.

385.2   HERBST, JOHANNES (1735-1812)
[Es ist vollbracht—Vergiss es nicht]

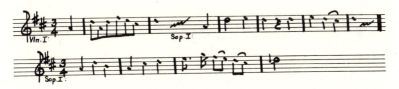

SSTB;Str.-*Allegro ma non troppo;Lebhaft.*-68m.-Hymn.

386   HERBST, JOHANNES (1735-1812)

386.1   [Blessed shalt thou be]

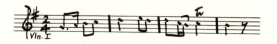

SSAB;Str.-G maj.-*Moderato.*-49m.-Deuteronomy 28:6; Jeremiah 31:34.

386.2   [Praise the Lord, o Jerusalem]

SSAB;Str.-D maj.-*Vivace.*-84m.-Psalm 147:12-14.

387.1   ROLLE, JOHANN HEINRICH (1718-1785)
        [Hab Dank, o Lamm!]

SSAB;Str.-F min.-*Moderato, con Sordini.*-50m.-Hymn119:6,7,9
(Freylinghausen).
From his *Saul* [See B XXXIII]
For another copy, see Herbst [473.5].

387.2   SCHULZ, JOHANN ABRAHAM PETER (1747-1800)
        [Gemeine! wie ist dir zu Muth]

SS;Str.-D maj.-*Adagio*-15m.-Hymn.
From his collection of hymns, no. 2. [See B XXXVIII]
For another copy, See Herbst [473.6].

387.3   ROLLE, JOHANN HEINRICH (1718-1785)
        [Weil ich Jesu Schäflein bin]

SSAB;Str.-A maj.-*Allegretto.*-111m.-Hymn 1179 (Louise v. Hayn).
From his *Saul*[See B XXXIII].

387.4   ROLLE, JOHANN HEINRICH (1718-1785)
        [Geliebtes Chor!]

SSAB;Str.-C maj.-*Affettuoso.*-48m.-Hymn.
From his *Saul* [See B XXXIII].

388   HERBST, JOHANNES (1735-1812) *Zur Einweihung des neuen
        Kirchensaales in Bethlehem am 20. May 1806*
        [Gott hat unter uns aufgerichtet]

SSAB;2Fl;2Hn;Str.-D maj.-*Mässig lebhaft.*-113m.-II.Corinther 5:19;
Hymn 1,3 (Gregor).

389   REICHARDT, JOHANN FRIEDRICH (1752-1814)

389.1   [Wohl deinem Volke]

SATB;2 Ob;2Bn;2Hn;Str;Fondam.-F maj.-*Allegretto.*-101m.
From his *Der 65te Psalm*, no. 2 [See B XXIX]
For another version, see Herbst [471.1].

389.2   [Frohlockt und jauchzet]

SSTB/SSAB;2Fl;2Bn;2Hn;Str.-C maj.-*Etwas lebhaft.*-183m.
Alternate text: *Du machst frolocken.*
From his *Der 65te Psalm,* no 5. [See B XXIX]
For another version, see Herbst [389.2b].

[389.2b] [Frohlockt und jauchzet]

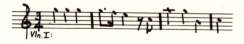

SSTB/SSAB;2Cl;2Bn;2Trpt*"clarini"*;Str.-C maj.-*Etwas lebhaft.*-183m.
From his *Der 65te Psalm,* no. 5. [See B XXIX]
For another version, see Herbst 389.2.

390   GRETRY, ANDRE (1741-1813)
       [Wiederholts mit süssen Tönen]

SATB/SS;2Cl;2Hn;Str.-C min.-*Andante.*-53m.-Hymn 122,1 (Gregor).

391 ´   NAUMANN, JOHANN GOTTLIEB (1741-1801) *aus Kapellmeister
        Naumanns Cora*

391.1   [Ach fändst du, Jesu]

B/SATB;Bn;Str.-F maj.-*Andante.*-80m.-Hymn.
Alternate text: *O Jesu, Quelle aller Gnaden.*

391.2   [Lass uns weiden]

SSAB;2Cl;2Hn;Str.-B-flat maj.-*Andante.*-104m.-Hymn 84 (Gregor).
See also Herbst 395.1.

392.1   WOLF, ERNST WILHELM (1735-1792) *Zum 25. Dec. 1794*
        [Singt ihr Erlösten]

SATB;2Hn;Str.-D maj.-*Munter.*-109m.-Hymn 581,4 (Neihser).

392.2   WOLF, ERNST WILHELM (1735-1792)
        [Ehre sey dem]

SATB;2 Ob;Str.-D maj.-*Allegro moderato.*-90m.-Johannis 11:25,26.

393   HERBST, JOHANNES (1735-1812)
        [Fürwahr, Er trug unsre Krankheit]

SSAB;Str.-F maj.-*Langsam.*-56m.-Jesaia 53:4,5.
See also Herbst 172 and Herbst 290.2.

394.1   [UNIDENTIFIED]
        [Du bist kommen zu dem Berge Zion]

SATB;Str.-B-Flat maj.-*Mässig.*-84m.-Ebräer 12:22-24.

394.2   HERBST, JOHANNES (1735-1812)
        [Unser Wandel ist im Himmel]

SATB;Str.-F min.-*Etwas langsam.*-61m.-Philipper 3:20.

394.3 [UNIDENTIFIED]
[Nun der Gott des Friedens]

SSTB;B-Flat maj. *Choralmässig.*-20m.-I.Thessalonicher 5:23,24.

395.1 NAUMANN, JOHANN GOTTLIEB (1741-1801)
[Lass uns weiden]

SSAB;Str;Cembalo.-B-Flat maj.-*Andante.*-104m.-Hymn 84 (Gregor).
See also Herbst 391.2.

395.2 GAMBOLD, JOHN (1760-1795)
[Jesus ward ein Mensch]

SS;Str.-F maj.-*Andante.*-8m.-Hymn 367,1 (Gregor).
See also Herbst 383.

396 HERBST, JOHANNES (1735-1812)
[Gott! man lobet dich—Gottes Brünnlein hat Wassers]

SSTB;bass.-C maj;F maj;C maj.-*Mässig.*-81m.-Psalm 65:2,3,10-14.

397 HOMILIUS, GOTTFRIED AUGUST (1714-1785)
[Für mich, o Herr]

SATB;2Fl;Str;keyboard.-C min.-*Traurig.*-45m.-Hymn.

398.1 GEBHARD, JOHANN GOTTFRIED (1755-)
[Ein Lämmlein geht]

SS;Fl;Vcl;Str;fig.bass.-G min.-*Largo.*-54m.-Hymn 118,1 (Gerhard).

398.2   GEBHARD, JOHANN GOTTFRIED (1755-)
[Ruhe sanft]

ST;Cl;Vcl;Str;Fondamento(fig.bass).-E-Flat maj.-*Lento. sempre
piano.*-119m.-Hymn.

399.1   GEBHARD, JOHANN GOTTFRIED (1755-) *Zum grossen
Sabbath 1781*
[Er ist um unsrer Missethat]

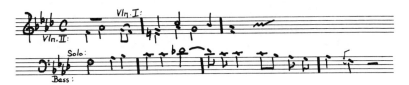

B/SATB;2Fl;Str;Fondam(fig.bass).-F min.-*Mesto.*-98m.-Jesaia 53:5.

399.2   GEBHARD, JOHANN GOTTFRIED (1755-)
[Ich stehe mit bewegtem Herzen]

S:Str;fig.bass.-B-Flat maj.-*Andante.*-84m.-Hymn.

400.1   GEISLER, JOHANN CHRISTIAN (1729-1815)
[Amen! Der Herr thue also]

SSAB;2Hn;Str;fig.bass.-D maj.-*Allegro ma non troppo.*-46m.-
Jeremia 28:6; I.Timotheum 1:17.
Alternate instrumental introductions, marked *"Introitus 1."*
and *"Introitus 2."*
2 copies.

400.2　GEISLER, JOHANN CHRISTIAN (1729-1815)
[Der Name des Herrn]

SSAB;2Hn;Str;fig.bass.-D maj.-*Allegro*.-60m.-Hiob 1:21.
2 copies.

400.3　RIESS, JOHANN HEINRICH (1768-1831)
[Erheb, o Chor, erhebe das Herz]

SSAB;2Hn;Str;fig.bass.-B-Flat maj.-*Allegro*.-81m.
2 copies.

400.4　ROLLE, JOHANN HEINRICH (1718-1785)
[Glückzu, glückzu, zu eurer Ruh!]

S;Str.-A maj.-*Grazioso, con Sordini*.-30m.-Hymn 1315 (Zinzendorf).
From his *Lazarus: "So schlummert auf rosen."*
2 copies.

401a　HERBST, JOHANN LUDWIG (1769-1824)
[Freuen und fröhlich]

S/SSAB;2Hn;Str;Organ obl.-C maj.-*Vivace*.-172m.-Psalm 70:5;
Hymn 446,3 (Gregor).
See also Herbst 401b.

401b HERBST, JOHANN LUDWIG (1769-1824)
[Freuen und fröhlich]

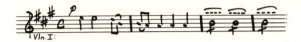

S/SSAB;Str.-A maj.-*Vivace.*-172m.-Psalm 70:5; Hymn 446,3 (Gregor).
See also Herbst 401a.

402 GEBHARD, JOHANN GOTTFRIED (1755-)
[Der heilge Geist vom Himmel]

S/SSAB;[2Fl;2Hn];Str;fig.bass.-G maj.-*Moderato.*-100m.-Hymn.
Separate flute and horn pts.

403.1 GEBHARD, JOHANN GOTTFRIED (1755-)
[Gelobet sey der Herr, der Gott]

SATB;2Trpt *"clarini"* or Hn;Str;Fondamento.-D maj.-*Allegro
maestoso.*-86m.-I.Chronica 17:36.

403.2 GEBHARD, JOHANN GOTTFRIED (1755-)
[Gross sind die Werke]

SATB;2Hn;Str.-C maj.-*Grave;Andante.*-38m.-Psalms 111:2; 66:8.

403.3   HAYDN, FRANZ JOSEPH (1732-1809)
         [Das Wort vom Kreuz]

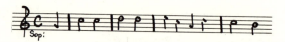

SATB;2 Ob;Bn;2Hn;Str;Vcl.-C maj.-*Allegro.*-129m.
Alternate text: *Volk Gottes! erzähle die Ehre.*
From *The Creation,* Part I, no. 14 [See B XVII].
Full score, followed by vocal score.

404.1   PETER, JOHN FREDERIK (1746-1813)
         [Jesus, unser Hirt]

SATB;2Fl;Bn;Str;Vcl.-G maj.-*Allegretto.*-53m.-Hymn.

404.2   MICHAEL, DAVID MORITZ (1751-1827)
         [Jesus nimmt sich]

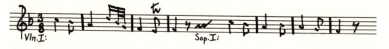

SSAB;Str.-F maj.-30m.

405   KUNZ, THOMAS ANTON (1759-   )
         [Lobet den Herrn, preiset]

SSTB;Str.-C maj.-*Poco Allegro.*-78m.-Psalm 96:4; Offenbarung 4:11.

406   BECHLER, JOHANN CHRISTIAN (1784-1857)
         [Gott ists, der in euch wirket]

SATB;2Hn;Str;Fondam;Organo.-E-Flat maj.-*Grave;Andante.*-
100m.-Philipper 2:3; Hymn.

407   BECHLER, JOHANN CHRISTIAN (1784-1857)
[Kommt, ach kommt]

SATB;2Hn;Str;Fondamento.-E-Flat maj.-*Lebhaft.*-76m.-
Hymn 713,2 (Zinzendorf).

408   WEBER, GOTTFRIED (1779-1839)
[Freuet euch des Herrn]

SSAB;Str.-E-Flat maj.-*Moderato.*-62m.-Psalm 33:1,4.

409   HERBST, JOHANNES (1735-1812)
[Da werdet ihr singen]

SSAB;Str.-C maj.-*Lebhaft nicht zu geschwind.*-66m.-Jesaia 30:29.

410   [UNIDENTIFIED]
[Kommt, lasset uns zum Herrn]

SATB;Str.-G maj.-*Moderato.*-64m.-Jeremia 50:5; Hymn 467,4
(Nitschmann).

411   GEBHARD, JOHANN GOTTFRIED (1755-)
       [Hallelujah! Lobet den Namen]

SATB/SATB;Str;Org.-D maj.-*Maestoso.*-109m.-Psalms 135:1-3; 96:7-9;
72:19.
Ms. marked "411a".

412.1 WOLF, ERNST WILHELM (1735-1792)
       [Was fühlet ihr]

SATB;2Hn;Str;Org(bass).-E-Flat maj.-*Moderato.*-96m.-Hymn.

412.2 WOLF, ERNST WILHELM (1735-1792)
       [Anbetung, Dank und Preis]

SATB;2Hn;Str.-E-Flat maj.-*Allegro.*-93m.

412.3 CUNOW, JOHANN GEBHARD (1760-1829)
       [O Jesu, nimm zum Lohn]

S;Str.-F maj.-*Langsam u. zärtlich.*-54m.-Hymn 639,5 (Gregor).
SSAB vocal score at end.
Alternate text: *Now sleep in peace and sweetest slumber.*

413.1 BECHLER, JOHANN CHRISTIAN (1784-1857)
       [Gross ist der Herr]

SATB;2Fl;2Hn;2Trpt*"Clarini"*;Str;Fond.-C maj.-*Allegro maestoso.*-
115m.-Psalm 48:2; Hymn.

413.2   BECHLER, JOHANN CHRISTIAN (1784-1857)
[Dank, Anbetung, Lob]

SATB;2Fl;2Hn;2Trpt*"Clarini"*;Str.-E-Flat maj.-*Maestoso.*-174m.-Hymn.

414.1   [UNIDENTIFIED]
[So spricht der Herr: Siehe, ich vertilge]

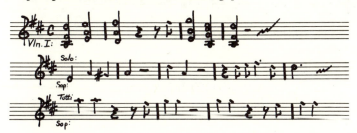

S/SATB;2Fl;2Hn;Str;Vcl;Organo.-D maj.-*Moderato.*-126m.-
Jesaia 44:22,23.

414.2   [UNIDENTIFIED]
[Danket dem Herrn, denn Er ist]

SATB;Fl;2 Ob;2Hn;2Trpt;Str;Organo.-D maj.-*Grave;Allegro.*-86m.-
I.Chronica 17:34.

415   GEBHARD, JOHANN GOTTFRIED (1755-)
        [Amen, Lob und Ehre]

SSAB;2Hn;Trpt;4Trb(SATB);Organo(fig.bass).-D maj.-*Maestoso.*-25m.-
Offenbarung 7:12,10.
See also Herbst 416a.2.

416a.1 HASSE, JOHANN ADOLPH (1699-1783)
        [Bereitet euer Herz]

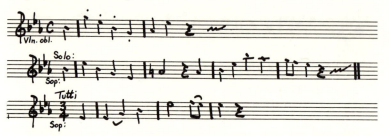

S/SATB;2Hn;Vln.obl;Str;keyboard.-E-Flat maj.-*Moderato;Vivace.*-
139m.-Hymn.
See also Herbst 416b.

416a.2 GEBHARD, JOHANN GOTTFRIED (1755-)
        [Amen, Lob und Ehre]

SSAB;fig.bass.-D maj.-*Maestoso.*-16m.-Offenbarung 7:12.
See also Herbst 415.

416b   HASSE, JOHANN ADOLPH (1699-1783)
        [Bereitet euer Herz]

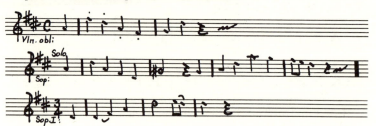

SSAB;Vln.obl;Str;keyboard.-D maj.-*Moderato;Vivace.*-139m.-Hymn.
See also Herbst 416a.1.

417   [UNIDENTIFIED]
       [Mache dich auf]

SATB;2Hn;2Trpt"*Clarini*";4Trb(SATB);Str.-C maj.-*Un poco Allegro.*-
99m.-Jesaia 60:1.

418.1   GEBHARD, JOHANN GOTTFRIED (1755-)
       [O verehrungswürdge Nacht]

B/SATB;Fl;2 Ob or Cl;2Bn;2Hn;Str;Organo(fig.bass).-G maj.-*Lebhaft,
doch in mässiger Bewegung.*-126m.-Hymn.

418.2   GREGOR, CHRISTIAN (1723-1801)
       [Mit fröhlichem Munde]

SATB;2Cl;2Hn;Str;Organo(fig.bass).-B-Flat maj.-*Andante.*-108m.-Hymn.
Arranged from C. W. Gluck's *Alceste.*

419   HAYDN, FRANZ JOSEPH (1732-1809)
       [O Wunder!]
       missing

420   HAYDN, FRANZ JOSEPH (1732-1809)
       [Es ist vollbracht]

SATB;2 Ob;Str.-B-Flat maj.-*Vivace.*-39m.
Adapted from Haydn's *The Creation,* Part II, no. 13 [See B XVII].
See also Herbst [420b].

[420b] HAYDN, FRANZ JOSEPH (1732-1809)
       [Es ist vollbracht]

SSTB;keyboard.-B-Flat maj.-*Vivace.*-37m.
Adapted from Haydn's *The Creation,* Pt. II, no 13 [See B XVII].
See also Herbst 420.
At end: a fragment from *The Creation,* Pt. I, no. 14 [See B XVII
and Herbst 403.3].

421   PETER, JOHN FREDERIK (1746-1813)
       [Da werdet ihr singen]

SATB/SSAB;2Fl;2Cl;Bn;2Hn;Str;Organo.-E-Flat maj.-*Lebhaft.*-83m.

422   GEISLER, JOHANN CHRISTIAN (1729-1815)
       [Ehre sey Gott in der Höhe]

SSAB/SSAB;2Fl;2Hn;Str;Org.-D maj.-*Allegro e maestoso.*-71m.-
Lucä 2:14.

423   MORTIMER, PETER (1750-1828)
       [Ehre sey Gott in der Höhe]

SATB/SSAB;2Trpt;Str;Fondamento(fig.bass).-D maj.-*Allabreve
Allegro.*-127m.-Lucä 2:14.

424   PETER, JOHN FREDERIK (1746-1813)
       [Kindlein bleibet bey ihm]
       Duetto

SS;2Fl;Bn;Str;Organo.-F maj.-*Mezzo Allegretto.*-99m.-I.Johannis 2:28;
I.Corinther 6:20.
SSTB vocal score on separate sheet, preceded by an unidentified
fragment marked *"L'Introduzione"* scored for 2 Hn, 2 Ob, 2 Bn.

425.1   BECHLER, JOHANN CHRISTIAN (1784-1857)
       [Gesalbeter Heiland]

SATB;2Cl;Bn;2Hn;Str;Organo.-E-Flat maj.-*Affettuoso.*-32m.-Hymn
439,1, var.(Schick).

425.2   BECHLER, JOHANN CHRISTIAN (1784-1857)
       [Sey Lob und Ehr]

SATB;2 Ob;2Hn;2Trpt;Timpani;Str;Organo.-D maj.-*Allegro moderato.*-
132m.-Hymn 1609,1-3 (Schaede).

426   BECHLER, JOHANN CHRISTIAN (1784-1857)
       [Bringe uns, Herr]

S/SATB;Str.-F maj.-*Langsam.*-82m.-Klaglieder 5:21.

427   LATROBE, CHRISTIAN IGNATIUS (1758-1836)
       [Was Othem hat]

SATB;[2Hn] ;Str.-D maj.-*Allegretto.*-58m.-Hymn.
Horn pts. on back of ms.

428a   GEBHARD, JOHANN GOTTFRIED (1755-)
       [Lob sey Christo]

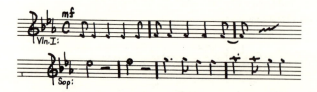

SATB;2Cl;2Hn;Trpt"*Clarino*";Str.-E-Flat maj.-*Vivace.*-131m.-Hymn 9
[*Liturgische Gesänge. . .,* 1793]
See Herbst 428b.

428b   GEBHARD, JOHANN GOTTFRIED (1755-)
       [Lob sey Christo]

SATB;Str;Organo.-D maj.-*Vivace.*-131m.-Hymn 9 [*Liturgische Gesänge. . .*, 1793]
See also Herbst 428a.

429.1   WOLF, ERNST WILHELM (1735-1792)
         [Gehet zu Seinen Thoren]

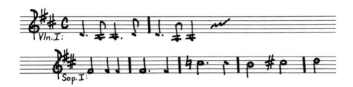

SATB;2Fl;2Hn;Str.-D maj.-*Allegro.*-119m.-Psalm 100:4,5.

429.2   WOLF, ERNST WILHELM (1735-1792)
         [Lobe den Herrn meine Seele, und was in mir]

SATB;Str.-B-Flat maj.-*Allegro.*-90m.-Psalm 103:1,2.

430.1   HERBST, JOHANN LUDWIG (1769-1824)
         [Wenn kleine Himmels-Erben]

S;Str/SSAB;Str.-G maj.-*Moderato con Sordini, sempre piano; Etwas langsamer.*-144m.-Hymn 1688,1 (Rothe).

430.2   HERBST, JOHANN LUDWIG (1769-1824)
         [Wenn Kinder die sterbliche Hütte]

S;Str.-C min.-*Andante.*-85m.-Hymn.
SATB vocal score on separate sheet.

431   NAUMANN, JOHANN GOTTLIEB (1741-1801)
[Heilig, heilig, heilig]

SATB;2Hn;Str/SS;2Fl;Bn;Organo.-E-Flat maj.-*Langsam u. andächtig.-*
123m.-Jesaia 6:3.

432.1   HERBST, JOHANNES (1735-1812)
[Es sollen wol Berge]

SSTB;Str.-G maj.-*Vivace.*-146m.-Jesaia 54:10; Hymn.

432.2   VAN VLECK, JACOB (1751-1831)
[Bleeding, suff'ring agonizing Jesus]

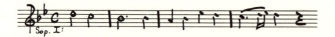

SSAB;Str.-B-Flat maj.-*Feyerlich.*-26m.-Hymn.

433.1   [UNIDENTIFIED]
[Kommt, wir wollen niederfallen]

SATB;[Vln.obl] ;Str.-C maj.-*Andante.*-64m.-Hymns 986,12 (Zinzendorf);
526,7 (Winkler).
Violin obbligato on separate sheet.
Alternate text: *Gott im unserm Fleisch erschienen.*

433.2   [UNIDENTIFIED]
[Hier sinkt o Lamm]

SATB;Str.-C maj.-*Quasi Allegro.*-46m.-Hymn 1090,1 (Schlicht).

433.3   MICHAEL, DAVID MORITZ (1751-1827)
[Wir sind Glieder]

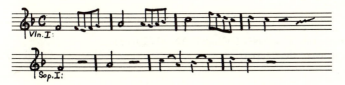

SSAB;Str.-F maj.-*Vergnügt.*-59m.-Epheser 5:30.

433.4   MICHAEL, DAVID MORITZ (1751-1827)
[Gott sey dir gnädig]

S/SSAB;Str.-F maj.-*Affettuoso.*-80m.

434.1   LATROBE, CHRISTIAN IGNATIUS (1758-1836)
[Mit deinem verdienstlichen Tod]

TS/SATB;Str.-D min.-*Largo.*-84m.-Hymn.

434.2   SOERENSEN, JOHANN (1767-1824)
[Selig alle, die im Herrn]

SATB;Str.-E maj.-*Andante.*-51m.-Hymn.
Alternate text: *Meine Leiche Jesu.*

435a.1 NAUMANN, JOHANN GOTTLIEB (1741-1801)
[Singet dem Herrn ein neues Lied. Die Gemeine]

SSTB;2Fl;Bn;2Hn;Str;Fondam.-F maj.-*In mässiger Bewegung.*-167m.-
Psalm 149:1-5.
See also Herbst 435b.1.

435a.2 GEISLER, JOHANN CHRISTIAN (1729-1815)
[Ich harre des Herrn]

SSTB;2Fl;Bn;Str.-G maj.-*Langsam mit Empfindung.*-46m.-Psalm 130:5,6.
See also Herbst 435b.2.

435b.1 NAUMANN, JOHANN GOTTLIEB (1741-1801)
[Singet dem Herrn ein neues Lied. Die Gemeine]

SSAB;Str.-F maj.-*In mässiger Bewegung.*-167m.-Psalm 149:1-5.

435b.2 GEISLER, JOHANN CHRISTIAN (1729-1815)
[Ich harre des Herrn]

SSAB;Str.-G maj.-*Langsam mit Empfindung.*-46m.-Psalm 130:5,6.

435b.3 GEISLER, JOHANN CHRISTIAN (1729-1815)
[Siehe, das ist Gottes Lamm]

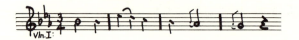

SSAB;Str.-E-Flat maj.-*Sehr langsam.*-100m.-Johannis 1:29.

436   PETER, JOHN FREDERIK (1746-1813)
    [Kommt danket dem Helden]

SSAB/SSAB;2Fl;2Hn;Str.-G maj.-*Vivace assai.*-35m.-Hymn 200,1,6
(Herrnschmidt).
Antiphonal presentation of text: Choir I-verse 1; Choir II-verse 6.

437   [UNIDENTIFIED]
    [Ehre sey Gottes Lamm]
    Passions-Gesang

SSAB;Str.-E-Flat;A-Flat;E-Flat;F min;B-Flat;E-Flat.-*Grave;Langsam;*
Nicht zu geschwind;Etwas langsam;Sanft;Munter, nicht zu langsam.-270m.

438.1   PETER, JOHN FREDERIK (1746-1813)
    [Bereitet euer Herz]

S/SATB;2Fl;Bn;2Hn;Str;Fondam;[Organo].-E-Flat maj.-*Maestoso;Vivace*
assai.-149m.-Hymn.
Organo pt. on separate sheet.

438.2   GAMBOLD, JOHN (1760-1795)
    [Macht hoch die Thür]

SSATB;2 Ob;2Trpt;Str;Fondam;[Organo].-D maj.-*Allegro maestoso.*-122m.
Hymn 39,1 (Weissel).
Organo pt. on separate sheet.

439   REICHARDT, JOHANN FRIEDRICH (1752-1814)
        [Seht ihr Erlöste]
        Quartetto

    SSTB solo;2Fl;2Bn;2Hn;Str;Vcl.solo.-F min.-*Poco Adagio.*-101m.
    From his *Trauer Cantata.* [See B XXX]
    2 copies.

440   HERBST, JOHANNES (1735-1812)
        [Du bist kommen zu dem Berge Zion]

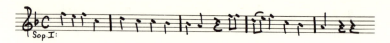

    SSAB;Str.-F maj.-*Mässig lebhaft.*-75m.-Ebräer 12:22-24.
    2 copies.

441   BECHLER, JOHANN CHRISTIAN (1784-1857)
        [Unsre Seel soll dich erheben]

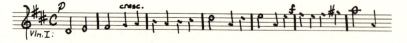

    SATB;2Fl;2Hn;2Trpt"*clarini*";Str;Organo.-D maj.-116m.-*Allegro
    maestoso.*-Hymn 583 (Louise v. Hayn).

442   BECHLER, JOHANN CHRISTIAN (1784-1857)
        [Die Gnade des Herrn Jesu]

    SATB;2Hn;Str;Fondam.-E-Flat maj.-*Feierlich.*-74m.-II.Corinther 13:13.
    In Herbst's book of texts: "*Zu meinem Geburtstage d. 23. July 1809.*"
    Hn. pts added above or below the score, as space permits.
    A second copy, without Hn. pts.

443   HERBST, JOHANNES (1735-1812)
        [Kindlein! bleibet bey Ihm]

SSAB;Str.-B-Flat maj.-*Mässig.*-105m.-I.Johannis 2:28; I.Corinther 6:20.

444   MICHAEL, DAVID MORITZ (1751-1827)
       [Kindlein, bleibt bey Jesu Christ]

S/SSAB;Str.-G maj.-*Andante.*-57m.-Hymn 1191 (Gregor).

445   HERBST, JOHANNES (1735-1812)
       [Wie lieblich, trostend]

SSAB;Str. C min.-*Affettuoso, Adagio.*-64m.-Hymn.

446.1 HERBST, JOHANNES (1735-1812)
       [So lange wir hienieden]

SSAB;Str.-F maj.-*Andante.*-74m.-Hymn.

446.2 HERBST, JOHANNES (1735-1812)
       [Hier bleiben Jesu]

SSAB;Str.-A maj.-*Larghetto.*-63m.

447   HERBST, JOHANNES (1735-1812)
       [Amen, Ruhm, Dank]

SATB;2Fl;2Hn;Str;Fondamento.-D maj.-*Allegro maestoso.*-85m.-Hymn.
Alternate text: *Lob sey Christo.*

448   BECHLER, JOHANN CHRISTIAN (1784-1857)
       [Hallelujah, Preis, Ehr]

SATB;2Fl;2Cl;2Bn;2Hn;2Trpt;Str;Fondamento.-C maj.-*Allegro
moderato.*-173m.-Hymn 258,2 (Zinzendorf).

449   HERBST, JOHANNES (1735-1812)
       [Der Herr ist unser König]

SATB;2Fl;2Hn;Str;Fondamento.-D maj.-*Allegro moderato.*-124m.-
Jesaia 33:22; Psalms 72:12,13; 117:2; 149:4; 115:12; 125:2.
See Herbst 96.4.
A second, unnumbered, copy marked by Herbst as the property of
"Chr. Fr. Schaaf".

450.1   BECHLER, JOHANN CHRISTIAN (1784-1857)
       [Preis und Dank und Ehre]

SATB;2 Ob.or Cl;2Hn;2Trpt;Str[Organo] ;fig. bass.-D maj.-
Allegro pomposo.-123m.-Hymn.
Organo pt. on separate sheet.
Above Herbst's signature: *"Episc. Fr. Unitas Fratrum def: Januarii*

quindecim. MDCCCXII" in another hand.
Alternate text: *Joyfull praise and adoration.*

450.2   BECHLER, JOHANN CHRISTIAN (1784-1857)
[Lob sey dir, Herr aller Dinge]

SATB;2Cl;2Hn;2Trpt*"clarini"*;Str;[Organo].-C maj.-*Moderato.-*
145m.-Hymn.
Organo pt. on separate sheet (incomplete).

451a   HERBST, JOHANNES (1735-1812)
[Freuet euch und seyd fröhlich]

SATB;2Cl;2Hn;Str;Fondamento.-C maj.-*Lebhaft, doch nicht zu
geschwind.*-124m.-Psalms 45:3; 104:2; 72:19.
See also Herbst 451b.

451b   HERBST, JOHANNES (1735-1812)
[Freuet euch und seyd fröhlich]

SSAB;2Cl;[2Hn];Str;Fondamento.-B-Flat maj.-*Lebhaft, doch nicht zu
geschwind.*-124m.-Psalms 45:3; 104:2; 72:19.
"Corni in B. Siehe No. 451a."

452   HERBST, JOHANNES (1735-1812)
[Hallelujah! lasst uns singen]

SATB;2Cl;Bn;2Hn;Str;Fondamento.-E-Flat maj.-*Moderato.*-126m.-Hymn.

453   PETER, JOHN FREDERIK (1746-1813)
[Singet ihr Himmel!]

SATB;2Fl;2Cl;2Bn;2Hn;2Trpt*"clarini"*;Str;Fondamento.-B-Flat maj.-
Allegro.-129m.-Hymn.
*"Meinem lieben Bruder Johannes Herbst freundschaftlichest dedicirt
von J.F.P."*

454   MICHAEL, DAVID MORITZ (1751-1827)
[Siehe, ich verkündige euch grosse Freude—Ehre sey Gott in der Höhe]

S;Str/SSTB;2Fl;2Cl;2Bn;2Trpt;Str;Fondamento.-D maj.-*Allegro.*-113m.-
Lucä 2:10,11,14.

455   GEBHARD, JOHANN GOTTFRIED (1755-)
[Ihre Seele gefiel Gott]

SATB;Str;keyboard.-A min.-*Andante molto, con Sordini.*-79m.-Hymn.

456   GEBHARD, JOHANN GOTTFRIED (1755-)
[Ach wiederholt mir Jesu]

SATB;2Fl;Str.-C min.-*Largo.*-77m.-Hymn 164 (Louise v. Hayn).

457   GEISLER, JOHANN CHRISTIAN (1729-1815) *Zum Pfingstfest in Herrnhut. 1800*
[Ehre sey Gott]

SSAB/SSAB;2Bn;2Hn;Str; Organo(bass).-E-Flat maj.-*Andante.-*
125m.-Hymn.

458   BECHLER, JOHANN CHRISTIAN (1784-1857)
[Ich will dem Herrn singen]

S/Fl.obl;Str/SATB;Organo.-C maj.-*Allegretto.*-134m.-Psalm 104:33;
Hymn 134,8 (Rist), Hymn 166,10 (C.R. von Zinzendorf); Tunes 168A,
185A (second part).
Psalm (solo) alternates with chorales (SATB).

459   ROLLE, JOHANN HEINRICH (1718-1785)
[Preis und Anbetung Ihm dem Herrn]

SATB;2Fl;2Cl;2Hn;Str;Fondam.-F maj.-*Vivace moderato; Vivace.*-93m.

460   GEISLER, JOHANN CHRISTIAN (1729-1815) *Zur Christnacht 1803*

460.1   [Wie heilig ist die Nacht]

SATB;Str.-G maj.-*Lieblich u. sehr mässig. Andante.*-29m.-Hymn.
"Melodie von Gregor, Text u. Accomp. von Geisler."
For alternate text, see Herbst 460.2.
Followed by incipit of chorale *Lob sey dir.*

460.2   [Holdseligs Gottes Kind]

SATB;Str.-G maj.-29m.-Hymn.
"Melodie von Gregor, Text u. Accomp. von Geisler."
For alternate text, see Herbst 460.1.

460.3   GEISLER, JOHANN CHRISTIAN (1729-1815)
         [Wenn wir unsern Lauf]

SSAB;Str.-E-Flat maj.-*Poco largo.*-100m.

461   HANDEL, GEORGE FREDERICK (1685-1759)
         [Siehe, das ist unser Gott]

SATB;Str.-E-Flat maj.-*Andante Larghetto.*-53m.-Jesaia 25:9.
See also Herbst 376.1.

462   PETER, SIMON (1743-1819)
        [O Anblick, der mir's Herze]

S;Str;keyboard.-C min.-*Affettuoso.*-33m.-Hymn 112 (Gregor).

463   GEISLER, JOHANN CHRISTIAN (1729-1815) *Oster Music*
        [Man singet mit Freuden]

SSAB;2Trpt*"clarini"*;Str.-D maj.-*Allegro moderato.*-39m.-
Psalm 118:15,16.

464   GEISLER, JOHANN CHRISTIAN (1729-1815)
        Zum Osterfest in Herrnhut 1802

464[.1] [Hallelujah, Heil und Preis]

SSAB/SSAB;2Fl;2Hn;Str;Organo(bass).-D maj.-*Andante maestoso.*-
41m.-Offenbarung 19:1.

464[.2] [Lobet unsern Gott]

T;Fl;Str;Organo(bass).-G maj.-*Andante.*-50m.-Offenbarung 19:5.

464[.3] [Lasset uns freuen]

SSAB/SSAB;2Fl;2Hn;Str;Organo(bass).-D maj.-*Vivace.*-71m.-
Offenbarung 19:7; 5:9; 1:18.

[465] GEBHARD, JOHANN GOTTFRIED (1755-   )

[465.1] [Ich will vor dem Herrn spielen]

SATB;Str.-D maj.-*Etwas lebhaft.*-58m.-Psalm 106:1.
Not entered in Herbst's book of texts.

[465.2] [Ich will den Namen]

SATB;Str.-G maj.-*Moderat.*-82m.
Not entered in Herbst's book of texts.

[465.3] [Freuet euch Gottes eures Heilands]

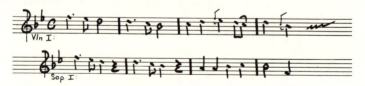

SSAB;Str.-B-Flat maj.-*Vivace.*-42m.
Not entered in Herbst's book of texts.

[466.1] GEISLER, JOHANN CHRISTIAN (1729-1815)
    [Die Gottes Seraphim—Heilig ist der Herr—Dank sey dem—Ehre dem
    Gotteslamm—Amen, Lob und Ehre]

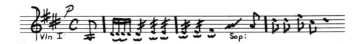

S recit;SATB/SATB;SA duet;SSAB;2Fl;2Hn;Str;Organ.-D maj;A maj;
E maj;A maj;D maj.-*Allegro troppo moderato;Allabreve maestoso;
Andante;troppo moderato;maestoso.*-186m.-Hymn 1600,1,2 (Gregor);
Jesaia 6:3; Offenbarung 7:12.
Not entered in Herbst's book of texts.

[466.2] [UNIDENTIFIED]
[Wie lieblich sind deine Wohnungen]

SSAB/SSAB;2Fl;2Hn;Str;Fondamento.-F maj.-*Allegretto quasi Allegro.
Angenehm u. munter.*-121m.-Psalm 84:2,3.
Not entered in Herbst's book of texts.

[467] GEISLER, JOHANN CHRISTIAN (1729-1815)
[Ich stehe mit bewegtem Herzen]

S[SAB];Str.-E-Flat maj.-*Affettuoso e lento. con Sordini.*-123m.
Geisler's solo setting, with choral pts. added by Herbst.
Alternate text (for choral setting): *Wir stehen mit bewegten Herzen.*
Not entered in Herbst's book of texts.

[468] GREGOR, CHRISTIAN (1723-1801)*Musik/zu denen in neuen
Liturgienbüchlein/No.1,12,15,u.21/onthaltenen Liturgien.*
[Performance directions are given on the title page]

[468.1] [Gelobet seyst du, der du thronest über Cherubim]
Liturgie No. 1.

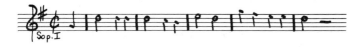

SSB;Str.-G maj.-177m.-Eingang 1 [*Liturgische Gesänge. . .*, 1793]
See Herbst 4.
Not entered in Herbst's book of texts.

[468.2] [Ehre sey Gott, dem Vater]
Liturgie No. 12

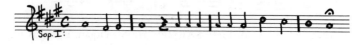

SSAB;fig.bass.-A maj.-85m.-Hymn 12: *Lobgesang zum Vater* [*Liturgische Gesänge. . .,1793*]
Contains sections for "*Liturgus*" and chorale incipits for "*Gemeine.*"
Not entered in Herbst's book of texts.

[468.3] [Lob und Preis und Ehre sey dem]
Lobgesang zum Sohne No. 15

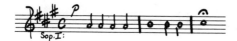

SSAB;fig.bass.-A maj.-98m.-Hymn 15 [*Liturgische Gesänge. . .1793*]
Contains sections for "*Liturgus*" and chorale incipits for "*Gemeine.*"
Not entered in Herbst's book of texts.

[468.4] [Ehre sey Gott dem heiligen Geiste]
Lobgesang zum heiligen Geiste No. 21

SSAB;fig.bass.-A maj.-100m.-Hymn 21 [*Liturgische Gesänge...,1793*]
Contains sections for "*Liturgus*" and chorale incipits for "*Gemeine.*"
Not entered in Herbst's book of texts.

[469.1] GREGOR, CHRISTIAN (1723-1801)
[Lobe den Herrn meine Seele]

SSAB;Str.-B-Flat maj.-*Mässig langsam.*-66m.-Psalm 103:2.
See also Herbst 22.1; Herbst 18.5.
Not entered in Herbst's book of texts.

[469.2] GREGOR, CHRISTIAN (1723-1801)
[Wie solln wir]

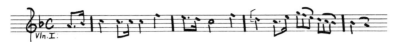

SSAB;Str.-F maj.-*Nicht geschwind.*-45m.-Psalm 116:12; I.Mose 32:10.
See also Herbst 29.2.
Not entered in Herbst's book of texts.

[470]   HERBST, JOHANNES (1735-1812)
        [Schlaf geliebten Bruder]

SSAB;Str.-F maj.-*Angenehm u. lieblich.*-81m.-Hymn.
Not entered in Herbst's book of texts.

[471]   REICHARDT, JOHANN FRIEDRICH (1752-1814)

[471.1] [Wohl deinem Volke]

SSTB;Str.-F maj.-*Allegretto.*-101m.
From his *Der 65te Psalm,* no. 2. [See B XXIX]
For another version, see Herbst 389.1.
Not entered in Herbst's book of texts.

[471.2] REICHARDT, JOHANN FRIEDRICH (1752-1814)
        [Hallelujah und Ehre]

SSTB;Str.-D maj.-*Feyerlich froh.*-16m.
Not entered in Herbst's book of texts.

[471.3] [UNIDENTIFIED]
        [Mein Jesu, der du vor dem Scheiden]
        Choral

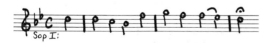

SSTB;Str.-B-Flat maj.-15m.-Hymn 1177,1,2 (Rambach); Tune 107B.
Not entered in Herbst's book of texts.

[472]   [UNIDENTIFIED]
        [Singet dem Herrn ein neues Lied. Sein Ruhm—Das Lied, das hier
        und droben tönt]

SSAB/SSAB;2Fl;2Hn;Str;Fondam.-D maj.-*Vivace moderato;Andante;
Gravitaetisch lebhaft.*-75m.-Jesaia 42:10; Hymn.
Not entered in Herbst's book of texts.

[473.1] GAMBOLD, JOHN (1760-1795)
        [Blutge Leiden]

SSAB;Str.-A min.-*Largo.*--54m.-Hymn 169,1 (C.L.Brau).
Ms. marked by Herbst as the property of "*Jac. van Vleck*".
Not entered in Herbst's book of texts.
For another copy, see Herbst 380.1.

[473.2] GAMBOLD, JOHN (1760-1795)
        [Ich seh in bangen Buss-Ideen]

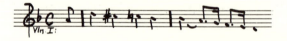

SSAB;Str.-D min.-*Lento sostenuto.*-28m.-Hymn 165,1 (C.R.v.Zinzendorf).
Ms. marked by Herbst as the property of "*Jac. van Vleck*".
Not entered in Herbst's book of texts.
For another copy, see Herbst 380.2.

[473.3] GAMBOLD, JOHN (1760-1795)
        [Todesblick, der mir mein Herz]

SSAB;Str.-G min.-*Largo espressivo.*-22m.-Hymn 169,2 (C.L.Brau).
Ms. marked by Herbst as the property of *"Jac. van Vleck".*
Not entered in Herbst's book of texts.
For another copy, see Herbst 380.3.

[473.4] GAMBOLD, JOHN (1760-1795)
[Deines Todes Trost]

SSAB;Str.-B-flat maj.-*Andante.*-50m.-Hymn 139,2 (Gregor).
Ms. marked by Herbst as the property of *"Jac. van Vleck".*
Not entered in Herbst's book of texts.
For another copy, see Herbst 380.4.

[473.5] ROLLE, JOHANN HEINRICH (1718-1785)
[Hab Dank, o Lamm!]

SSAB;Str.-F min.-*Moderato, con Sordini.*-50m.-Hymn 119,6,7,9
(Freylinghausen).
From his *Saul* [See B XXXIII].
Ms. marked by Herbst as the property of *"Jac. van Vleck".*
Not entered in Herbst's book of texts.
For another copy, see Herbst 387.1.

[473.6] SCHULZ, JOHANN ABRAHAM PETER (1747-1800)
[Gemeine! wie ist dir zu Muth]

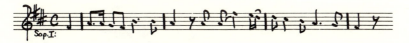

SS;Str.-D maj.-*Adagio.*-15m.-Hymn.
From his collection of hymns, no. 2 [See B XXXVIII].
Ms. marked by Herbst as the property of *"Jac. van Vleck".*
Not entered in Herbst's book of texts.
For another copy, see Herbst 387.2.

B. EXTENDED WORKS IN THE
JOHANNES HERBST COLLECTION

I   QUANTZ, JOHANN JOACHIM (1697-1773)
    Vorspiel zu Ramler's Hirten bey der Krippe,
    von H. Quanzen hinzugefügt.

2Fl,2 Ob;Str;Organ(bass).-G maj.-*Pastorale.*-125m.

AGRICOLA, JOHANN FRIEDRICH (1720-1774)
[Die Hirten bey der Krippe zu Bethlehem]

Full score, 72p: 1-8, overture; 9-72, oratorio.-20x33 cm.
At end: *"Soli Deo gloria. Ser. Mense Majo 71. J. F. Kehl."*

II BACH, CARL PHILIPP EMANUEL (1714-1788)
    Die Israeliten in der Wüste/ ein Oratorium/ in Musik gesetzt/ von Carl
    Philipp Emanuel Bach.

    Full score, 81p.-21x33 cm.

III BENEVOLI, ORAZIO (1605-1672)
    Sanctus/ et/ Dona nobis pacem/ a/ 2 Trombe/ Tamburi/ 2 Oboi/
    2 Violini/ Viola/ 1 Chori reali/ Organo/ del/ Sigr. Benevoli.

    Full score, 18p; Vocal score, 5p.-21x34 cm.

IV GRAUN, KARL HEINRICH (1704-1759)
    Duetti/ Terzetti/ Sestetti/ ed/ alcuni Chori/ Delle Opere/ del Signore/
    Carlo Enrico Graun/ Già Mastro di Capella di Sua Maestà/ il Re di
    Prussia.

    6 vol., vol.1-4: 33 duets, 9 trios, 2 sextets, 10 choruses.-Full score.-
    18x24 cm; vol.5: Plot synopses of Graun's operas.-18x24 cm; vol.6:
    book of texts, Italian and English.-10½x17 cm.

V   GRAUN, KARL HEINRICH (1704-1759)
     Missa/ Kyrie cum Gloria/ di Sig. Graun.

     Full score, 39p.-18x24 cm.

VI   GRAUN, KARL HEINRICH (1704-1759)
     Te Deum Laudamus/ posto in Musica/ dal/ Sig. Carlo Enrico Graun.

     Full score, 71p.-18x24 cm.
     Pts: Fl.I, Ob.I, Fondamento (all incomplete).

VII HANDEL, GEORGE FREDERICK (1685-1759)
     *Chorus's in/ Messiah/ an/ Oratorio/ set to Musick by/ Mr. Handel/
     To which are added/ His additional Alterations.*

     Full score, 87p.-21x34 cm.
     Pts. Canto, Alto, Tenore, Basso; Oboe I,II; Tromba I; Violino I,II,
     Viola, Fondamento.-22x36½ cm.

VIII HASSE, JOHANN ADOLPH (1699-1783)
     Oratorium/ Conversione/ di St. Agostino/ del/ Sigr. Hasse.

     Full score, 42p.-21x34 cm.

IX   HASSE, JOHANN ADOLPH (1699-1783)
     Il Cantico/ De' Tre Fanciulli/ Oratorio/ del/ Sigr. Giov. Adolfo Hasse.

     Full score, 110p.-18x23 cm.

X   HASSE, JOHANN ADOLPH (1699-1783)
     Ex Oratorio/ La Caduta/ di Gerico/ di Hasse.

     Full score, 42p.-18x24 cm.

XI   HASSE, JOHANN ADOLPH (1699-1783)
     Due Chori/ con una Aria/ ex Oratorio/ Giuseppe Liberato/ di Hasse.

     Full score, 22p.-18x24 cm.

XII HASSE, JOHANN ADOLPH (1699-1783)
     Magdalena/ Oratorium/ del Sigr. Giov. Adolfo Hasse.

     Full score, 45p.-18x24 cm.

XIII   HASSE, JOHANN ADOLPH (1699-1783)
*I Pellegrini/ al Sepolcro/ Di nostro Salvatore/ del Sigr. Hasse./
Oratorio/ cantando nella regia Elettoral Capella/ di Dresda La
Sera del Venerdi Santo/ MDCCXLII.*

Full score, 93p.-18x24 cm.

XIV   HASSE, JOHANN ADOLPH (1699-1783)
*Sant Elena/ al Calvario/ Oratorio/ posto in Musica/ del/ Sig. Giovan
Adolf Hasse.*

Full score, 74p.-21x34 cm.

XV   HASSE, JOHANN ADOLPH (1699-1783)
Te Deum Laudamus/ posto in Musica/ del Sigr. Giov. Ad. Hasse.

Full score, 78p.-18x24 cm.

XVI   HASSE, JOHANN ADOLPH (1699-1783)
Te Deum laudamus/ del Sig. G. A. Hasse.

Full score, 51p.-18x24 cm.
Pts: Canto I, Alto, Tenore, Basso; Violino I,II, Viola, Violoncello.

XVII   HAYDN, FRANZ JOSEPH (1732-1809)
The Creation

Pts: Soprano, Tenore, Basso.-16x23½ cm.

XVIII   HAYDN, FRANZ JOSEPH (1732-1809)
*Joseph Haydens/ Passions Music/ zum/ Stabat Mater/ mit einer/
deutschen Parodie.*

Full score, 37p.-18x24 cm.-German text.

XIX   HERBST, JOHANN LUDWIG (1769-1824)
*Gedancken/ bey dem Heimgang/ des d. 12 Novber. 1786 in Niesky/
entschlafnen Kindes/ Sam. Heinr. Herbst/ dem Andenken desselben
gewidmet/ von seinem Bruder/ Joh. Ludw. Herbst./ Niesky d. 13ten
Jan:/ 1787.*

Full score, 46p.-18x24 cm.

XX   HILLER, JOHANN ADAM (1728-1804)
*Vierstimmige/ Motetten und Arien/ in Partitur,/ von verschiedenen
Componisten/ zum/ Gebrauche der Schulen und anderer Gesangs-
liebhaber/ gesammlet und herausgegeben/ von Johann Adam Hiller.*

5 vols., *Erster Theil:* Soprano pt. 5p(incomplete).-22x28 cm.
   Zweyter Theil: Alto pt., 8p(incomplete); Basso pt., 11p.-22x28 cm.
   Dritter Theil: Score, 46p; Alto pt., 15p;Tenore pt., 15p.-18x24 cm.
   Vierter Theil: Score, 46p; Canto, Alto, Tenore, Basso pts.-18x24 cm.
   ?Theil: Score, 57p.-18x22 cm; Canto pt., 5p(incomplete).-22x28 cm.

XXI   HIMMEL, FRIEDRICH HEINRICH (1765-1814)
Der 146te Psalm/ componirt/ von Himmel

Full score, 86p.-18x24 cm.

XXII HOMILIUS, GOTTFRIED AUGUST (1714-1785)
*Passions Canatae/ nach der Poesie/ der Herrn Buschmann/ componirt
von/ Gottfried August Homilius/ Cantor und Music-Director/ an der
Kreuz-Kirche zu Dresden.*

Full score, 116p.-18x24 cm.

XXIII JOMMELLI, NICOLA (1714-1774)
Oratorium/ La Passione/ di/ Gesu Christo/ del Sig. Jomelli.

Full score, 90p.-21x35 cm.

XXIV KNECHT, JUSTIN HEINRICH (1752-1817)
*Wechselgesang/ der/ Mirjam und Debora/aus dem Zehnten Gesange
der Klopstockischen/ Messiade/ in Music gesezt/ von/ Justin
Heinrich Knecht.*

Keyboard-vocal score, 21p.-18x24 cm.

XXV   LATROBE, CHRISTIAN IGNATIUS (1758-1836)
Cantata/ performed at the Opening/ of the Chapel/ of the/ United

Brethren/ at/ Fairfield in Lancashire/ July 9th 1785/ composed by C. I. La Trobe.

Full score, 62p.-18x24 cm.

XXVI   LATROBE, CHRISTIAN IGNATIUS (1758-1836)
The/ Dawn of Glory/ a Hymn/ on the Bliss of the/ Redeemed/ at the last Day/ set to Music/ by/ C. I. Latrobe./ adapted for the Pianoforte and Voices.

Piano-vocal score, 58p.-19x25 cm.

XXVII   MOZART, WOLFGANG AMADEUS (1756-1791)
Hymne an die Gottheit/ von W. A. Mozart.

Full score, 34p.-19x22 cm; Pts: Soprano, Alto, Tenore, Basso; Violini I,II,Viola,Violoncello; Organo.-18x24 cm; Flauto, Clarino I,II.-14½x23 cm.

XXVIII   PERGOLESI, GIOVANNI BATTISTA (1710-1736)
Missa/ del Sigr. G. B. Pergolesi/ Kyrie cum Gloria.

Full score, 36p.-21x34 cm.

XXIX   REICHARDT, JOHANN FRIEDRICH (1752-1814)
Der 65te Psalm/ in Musick gesetzt/ von/ Joh. Fr. Reichardt.

Full score, 78p.-18x24 cm.

XXX   REICHARDT, JOHANN FRIEDRICH (1752-1814)
Trauer Cantata/ auf den Tod Friedrichs II/ König in Preussen/ componirt/von/ Joh. Fr. Reichardt.

Full score, 68p.-18x24 cm.-Latin and English texts.

XXXI   REICHARDT, JOHANN FRIEDRICH (1752-1814)
Weinachts-Cantilene/ von/ Matthias Claudius/ in Musik gesezt/ von Johann Friedrich Reichardt/ Königl. Preuss. Capellmeister.

Full score, 82p; Pts: *Coro I,* Soprano, Alto, Tenore, Basso; *Coro II,* Canto I, Alto; Violino I,II, Viola, Basso e Violoncello.-18x24 cm.

XXXII   ROLLE, JOHANN HEINRICH (1718-1785)
Die Befreyung Israels/ ein musicalisches Drama/in Musik gesezet/ von/ Joh. Heinr. Rolle.

Keyboard-vocal score, 57p; Pts: Soprano, Alto, Tenore, Basso.-18x24 cm.

XXXIII ROLLE, JOHANN HEINRICH (1718-1785)
[Fourteen choruses]

Nos. 1-9, from *Saul*; nos. 10-14, from *Lazarus*.
Pts: Soprano (2), Alto I (2), Alto II, Tenore, Basso (2); Violino I,
II, Viola, Violoncello.

XXXIV ROLLE, JOHANN HEINRICH (1718-1785)
Aus Rollens Oratorio:/ Lazarus.

2 vols., vol. 1: 1. *Heiliger verlass ihn nicht*, 2. *Heilige Stätte, wo
entschlafene Brüder*; vol.2: 1. *Sanft und still schläft unser
Freund*, 2. *Mein stiller Abend ist gekommen*, 3. *Preiss dem Erwecker.*-
Full score.-18x24 cm.

XXXV ROLLE, JOHANN HEINRICH (1718-1785)
Leiden Jesu/von/ Joh. Heinr. Rolle.

Full score, 174p.-18x24 cm; Pts: Soprano, Alto, Tenore, Basso;
Coro II: Canto I, II, Alto, Basso; Violino I, II, Viola,
Violoncello.-20x23 cm.

XXXVI SCHMIEDT, SIEGFRIED (c.1756-1799)
Die Feyer/ des achtzehnden Jahrhunderts

Pts: Canto I, II, Tenore, Basso.

XXXVII SCHULZ, JOHANN ABRAHAM PETER (1747-1800)
Athalia

Keyboard-vocal score, incomplete.-16½x20 cm; Pts: Alto, Tenor, Basso
(incomplete); Oboe or Flute I, II, Fagotto I, II; Corno I, II;
Tromba I, II; Timpani; Violino I, Viola, Violoncello.-20x33 cm;
Coro II: Canto I, II, Alto, Basso.-16½x20 cm.

XXXVIII SCHULZ, JOHANN ABRAHAM PETER (1747-1800)
Hymne/ di Schulz

12 compositions-Pts: Alto; Flauto I, II; Corno I, II; Violino I, II,
Viola, Fondamento.-18x24 cm.

XXXIX SCHULZ, JOHANN ABRAHAM PETER (1747-1800)
*Maria und Johannes/ ein/ Passions-Oratorium/ componirt/ von/
J. A. P. Schulz.*

Full score, 86p.-18x24 cm; Pts: *Coro II*: Canto I, II, Alto, Basso.-18x24 cm; Violino I, II, Viola, Violoncello.-20x33 cm.

XL   TÜRK, DANIEL GOTTLOB (1756-1813)
Die Hirten/ bey der Krippe zu Bethlehem/ in Musik gesetzt/ von Daniel Gottlob Türk.

Keyboard-vocal score, 16p.-18x24 cm.

XLI   WOLF, ERNEST WILHELM (1735-1792)
Wolfs Ostercantate

Pts: Soprano I, II, Tenore, Basso; *Coro II*: Soprano I, II, Tenore, Basso; Oboe I (and Flauto traverso); Corno I, II; Trombe I, II, III; Tympano; Violino I, II, Viola, Fondamento.-21x23 cm.

XLII   WOLF, ERNST WILHELM (1735-1792)
Quatro/ di Sigr. E. W. Wolf.

SSTB;2Ob;2Hns;Str.-D maj.-*Allegro.*-161m.
Full score.-21x36 cm.

XLIII   WOLF, ERNST WILHELM (1735-1792)
[Auf der Lufte]

SSTB;Fl;2Hn;Str,-F maj.-*Allegro.*-170m.
From the *Ostercantate.* [See B XLI]

XLIV   PERGOLESI, GIOVANNI BATTISTA (1710-1736)
[Stabat Mater]

Score (SA;Str), incomplete.-16p.-21x34cm.-Latin text.
Pts: Soprano I, II, Tenore, Basso; Oboe or Flauto I, II; Violino I, II, Viola, Violoncello.-20x33cm.-German text: *Jesus schwebt am Kreuze.* Arranged by Johann Adam Hiller.

XLV   [UNIDENTIFIED]
Singstücke u. Motetten

22 compositions
Vocal score.-39p.-18x24 cm.
Pts: *Coro I*, Canto II, Tenore, Basso; *Coro II*, Canto I, II, Alto, Basso.-18x24 cm.

C. MISCELLANEOUS SCORES IN THE
JOHANNES HERBST COLLECTION

I   [Book of keyboard pieces (gigues, marches, minuets, murkeys, polonaises, sonatas)]

       Mostly anonymous; some works attributed to Corelli, Handel, Haydn, Hasse.
       Bound volume, 144p.-16x20 cm.obl.

II   *Lieder zum Singen am Clavier*

       152 sacred songs by John Gambold, J.A.P. Schulz, Herbst, and others.
       Bound volume, 177p.-16x20 cm.obl.

III   *Sammlung alter und neuer Sing Weisen zum Bruder-Gesang*

       Book of chorales.-melody and figured bass.
       Bound volume, 269p.(unfinished).-16x20 cm.obl.

IV   [Seven sacred songs for soprano with keyboard]

       Compositions by Gluck (3), Handel (1), and Sacchini (3).
       Unbound volume, 15p.(incomplete).-18x24 cm.

INDEX OF COMPOSERS

Agricola, Johann Friedrich
  A: 120.5
  B: I
Antes, John
  A: 366; 367; 368; 369

Bach, Carl Philipp Emanuel
  A: 219
  B: II
Bechler, Johann Christian
  A: 406; 407; 413; 425; 426; 441; 442;
  448; 450; 458
Benevoli, Orazio
  B: III
Bruiningk, Heinrich von
  A: 217.1

Corelli, Arcangelo
  C: I
Cruse, ? G. D.
  A: 188
Cunow, Johann Gebhard
  A: 412.3

Freydt, Johann Ludwig
  A: 197; 199; 201; 202; 203; 207; 208;
  211; 213.1,2,3; 213.2b; 214a; 214b;
  231; 232; 233; 234; 235; 236; 237;
  238; 239; 240; 241; 242; 243; 245;
  246; 248; 251; 254; 255.1; 256; 260;
  262; 263; 265; 268; 271; 272b; 291b;
  293; 293b; 294.1; 296; 305; 308; 309;
  310; 311; 312; 314; 315.1; 317; 319;
  322.1; 329; 357.1; 359.3

Gambold, John
  A: 282.3; 307; 359.1; 380; 383; 395.2;
  438.2; [473.1,2,3,4]
  C: II
Gebhard, Johann Gottfried
  A: 298.3; 378; 379; 398; 399; 402;
  403.1,2; 411; 415; 416a.2; 418.1; 428;
  455; 456; [465]
Gehra, August Heinrich
  A: 108; 156; 225.1; 226; 298.1,2; 327
Geisler, Christian Gottfried
  A: 49; 117.1; 164; 346
Geisler, Johann Christian
  A: 12; 20; 39; 40; 42; 43; 45; 47; 48;
  51; 53.2[b]; 56; 57; 58; 60; 61.1; 63;
65; 67; 68; 69; 70; 76; 77; 79; 80; 83;
85; 87; 88; 90; 91.1; 92; 93; 95;
96.6,7; 96[b]; 97.1; 100; 101; 103;
106; 107; 109.3,4,5,6; 112; 117; 118;
120.1,1b; 122.3,4; 124; 125; 127[.3,4];
128; 131; 133a; 133b; 136; 137; 139;
140; 143; 145; 148a; 148b; 149; 150;
151; 152; 155; 157; 160; 162; 163;
166; 167; 170.1; 171; 174; 175; 177;
177b; 185; 186; 189b; 190b; 194; 198;
206; 210; 212; 217.3,4; 220; 221;
222a; 222b; 223; 225.2,3; 228; [228a];
244b; 282.1b; 295; 297; 299; 301.2;
302.2; 304; 306; 316.1; 326; 343; 344;
345; 349; 350; 358; 400.1,2; 422;
435a.2; 435b.2,3; 457; 460; 463; 464;
[466.1]; [467]
Gluck, Christoph Willibald
  A: 357.3; 418.2
  C: IV
Graun, Karl Heinrich
  A: 23.2,3; 42.3; 47.2; 57; 67.4;
  104.1,2,5; 120.6; 164.4; 192.1; 249
  B: IV; V; VI
Gregor, Christian
  A: 1; 2; 3; [3b]; 4; 5; 6a; 6b; 7; 8; 9;
  10; 11.4; 13; 14; 15; 16; 17; 18; 19;
  21; 22, 23, 24; 25; 26; 27; 28; 29; 30;
  32; 33; 34; 35; 36.7; 37; 38; 39.4; 41;
  43; 46; 47.2; 49; 50; 53.1,2; 54; 55;
  59; 61; [62]; 64; 65.3; 66; 67.1; 72;
  73; 74; 80.5,6; 81.1,3,4,5,6,8; 91.1;
  96.3; 96[b].3,8; 97.4,5,6,8,11; 99.1;
  100.1; 102.6,8; 114; 127[.1,2,4]; 135.3;
  136.2; 138; 217.3; 250; 264[.3]; 280;
  286b; 341.2; 418.2; 460.1,2; [468];
  [469]
Gretry, Andre
  A: 390
Grimm, Johann Daniel
  A: 215; 216; 224.3; 348

Handel, George Frederick
  A: 96.5; 104.4,6; 204.2; 225.2; 290.1;
  347; 376.1; 377; 461
  B: VII
  C: I; IV
Hasse, Johann Adolph
  A: 158; 161; 165.2; 170.2; 218; 283;
  416a.1; 416b

INDEX OF TITLES
IN THE CONGREGATION MUSIC

Date Due